Praise for

Explore the National Marine Sanctuaries with Jean-Michel Cousteau

"Wonderful and illuminating..."

"This book series gives us deeply felt and profound insight into our country's amazing National Marine Sanctuaries. They are wonderful and illuminating volumes that show the sanctuaries' great beauty and awe. There is an urgent need for the world to learn about these momentous marine sanctuaries and how to protect them. I thank my dear friend, Jean-Michel Cousteau, and Ocean Futures Society, for calling attention to the care of these beautiful marine sanctuaries in our time of extreme need. Jean-Michel is the authoritative servant on the sea for our generation and future generations. This incredible series will be beneficial in getting the word out about the importance of protecting our oceans and the marine life that call it home."

–Robert Lyn Nelson
Artist/Environmentalist

"Easy for everyone to grasp..."

"Marine sanctuaries represent the most special places in the ocean. We cannot sustain the ocean without first sustaining our sanctuaries. But like all things in the ocean, they are beneath the surface and invisible to almost everyone. Jean-Michel, through his films and this book series, gives these life and makes the ocean visible and tangible. He is a keen observer of nature and a storyteller about the ocean. He adds a depth of understanding and interpretation that is easy for everyone to grasp."

–Daniel J. Basta
Past Director
NOAA's Office of National Marine Sanctuaries

"An undoubted 'treasurehouse'..."

"Jean-Michel Cousteau and Ocean Futures Society have set themselves the task of communicating the beauty of the ocean and the necessity of protecting it to the widest possible audience. Through stunning photography and superbly succinct writing, Explore the National Marine Sanctuaries with Jean-Michel Cousteau does just that. This wonderful book series shows how very precious the USA's National Marine Sanctuaries are, and what a huge contribution the sanctuaries make to our knowledge and understanding of the underwater world. The series is also very timely in light of the past events in the Gulf of Mexico which show how vulnerable the marine environment still is. Oil spillages do not respect marine sanctuaries any more than forest fires respect the boundaries of National Parks.

But without even the protection that the National Marine Sanctuaries offer, America's marine biodiversity—and the public knowledge and appreciation of it—would be the poorer. Those of us whose lives revolve around the protection of wildlife on land, rather than the marine environment, can only admire and envy Jean-Michel's extraordinary success in conserving, communicating and educating. Genuine environmentalists like Jean-Michel know that we need a truly holistic approach to the conservation of wildlife on land and sea. This book series is an undoubted 'treasure-house' and I have no hesitation in recommending it to all who love wildlife and wish to understand better how to redress the terrible imbalance between Man and Nature."

–Simon Cowell, MBE FRGS MCIJ
Founder, Wildlife Aid;
Producer and Presenter, Wildlife SOS, United Kingdom

"Beautiful and moving.."

"Jean-Michel Cousteau and his team have put together an amazing series of books dedicated to the undersea world on which we depend. This is the first time anyone has truly captured the experience of diving America's underwater treasures, the entire national marine sanctuary system. I cannot tell you how truly beautiful and moving a series this is. After spending time with this book, I am even more proud of America's commitment to protect our National Marine Sanctuaries."

–Jeff Mora
Los Angeles Lakers, Executive Chef,
Board Member, National Marine Sanctuary Foundation
International Advisory Board Member, Ocean Futures Society

"Compelling stories and magnificent images..."

"National Marine Sanctuaries are not only extraordinary places to visit, they are also one of our most powerful tools in ocean conservation. Explore the National Marine Sanctuaries with Jean-Michel Cousteau provides an underwater roadmap through the Sanctuaries with compelling stories and magnificent images. For those fortunate enough to have visited Sanctuaries, these books are the perfect way to preserve the memories. For those who have not, they are the next best thing to being there. Most importantly, Explore the National Marine Sanctuaries with Jean-Michel Cousteau teaches us that by protecting National Marine Sanctuaries we help protect the world-ocean...and ourselves."

–Bob Talbot
Chairman of the Board,
National Marine Sanctuary Foundation;
Board of Directors, Sea Shepherd Conservation Society,
Filmmaker and Photographer

Other Titles

by Jean-Michel Cousteau

*Explore the Southeast National Marine Sanctuaries
with Jean-Michel Cousteau*
Jean-Michel Cousteau

*Explore the West Coast National Marine Sanctuaries
with Jean-Michel Cousteau*
Jean-Michel Cousteau

*Explore the Northeast National Marine Sanctuaries
with Jean-Michel Cousteau*
Jean-Michel Cousteau

My Father, the Captain: My Life With Jacques Cousteau
Jean-Michel Cousteau and Daniel Paisner

Orcas: Spirits of the Sea
Dominique Sérafini and Jean-Michel Cousteau

Videos

Jean Michel Cousteau's Ocean Adventures:
Voyage to Kure
Sharks at Risk
Gray Whale Obstacle Course
America's Underwater Treasures, Parts 1 & 2
Return to the Amazon
Sea Ghosts
Call of the Killer Whale

My Father, the Captain: Jacques-Yves Cousteau

explore
the Pacific Islands
National Marine Sanctuaries
WITH JEAN-MICHEL COUSTEAU

HAWAIIAN ISLANDS HUMPBACK WHALE / AMERICAN SAMOA / PAPAHĀNAUMOKUĀKEA MONUMENT

OCEAN PUBLISHING

FRONT COVER: Céline Cousteau swims with spinner dolphins in Hawaii.
PHOTO CREDIT: Carrie Vonderhaar, Ocean Futures Society.
BOOK COVER, LAYOUT AND DESIGN: Nate Myers, Wilhelm Design
EDITING: Dr. Maia McGuire

Ocean Publishing is an imprint of Square One Publishers, Inc.

Square One Publishers
115 Herricks Road
Garden City Park, NY 11040
(516) 535-2010 • (877) 900-BOOK
www.squareonepublishers.com

Names: Cousteau, Jean-Michel, author.
Title: Explore the Pacific Islands National Marine Sanctuaries : HAWAIIAN
   ISLANDS HUMPBACK WHALE / AMERICAN SAMOA / PAPAHANAUMOKUAKEA
MONUMENT /
   with Jean-Michel Cousteau.
Description: 2nd edition. | Garden City Park, NY : Square One Publishers,
   [2017] | Series: Explore the National Marine Sanctuaries with Jean-Michel
   Cousteau | Previous edition: 2014. | Includes bibliographical references
   and index.
Identifiers: LCCN 2016033534 | ISBN 9780982694046 (paperback : alk. paper)
Subjects: LCSH: Marine parks and reserves—Islands of the Pacific. | Marine
   parks and reserves—Pacific Ocean.
Classification: LCC QH91.75.P16 C68 2017 | DDC 333.91/641609164—dc23 LC record available
at https://lccn.loc.gov/2016033534

Copyright © 2017 by Ocean Futures Society

ISBN 978-0-9826940-4-6

Printed in the United States of America

10   9   8   7   6   5   4   3   2   1

Contents

To all those who never give up,
who see the impossible and make it possible.
Ocean Futures Society's past, present and future teams
represent a wide range of devoted ocean conservationists who love the sea
and put in long hours—on expedition, in the editing room,
in the classroom, or at the office computer. They play different roles,
do 150 percent of what they're asked, and are paid mostly in
the knowledge that their work makes a difference.
That is, after all, the great adventure.

Foreword

Jean-Michel Cousteau's love of the ocean and the desire to protect it began as a boy, inspired by living on the edge of the Mediterranean Sea and sharing underwater adventures in the Atlantic, Pacific and Indian oceans with his parents, brother, and other pioneering ocean explorers aboard the legendary ship, *Calypso*. Ask him what it is about the ocean that has captured his heart and mind, and he might tell you of face-to-face encounters with curious fish, squid and great white sharks or the joy of gliding through forests of kelp or being underwater at night surrounded by a living cosmos of bioluminescent creatures. He could say how rewarding it is to be an explorer, to be the first to see places and meet forms of life in the sea that have not yet been given names. And, he would likely encourage you to go experience such things for yourself in places such as those celebrated in this volume and others that follow.

Cousteau's deep commitment to the National Marine Sanctuary Program stems from understanding how important the sanctuaries are as a means of protecting the nation's natural, historic and cultural heritage. Like national parks and wildlife management areas on the land, marine sanctuaries safeguard healthy systems and help restore those that have been harmed. While some observers believe the ocean should be able to take care of itself, many species prized for food or sport have declined by 90 percent or more in a few decades. Low oxygen areas, "dead zones," are proliferating, and sea grass meadows and coral reefs are diminishing. Major changes, most not favorable to humankind, are underway, and the sanctuaries can give stressed systems and species a break. We need the oceans, and now the oceans need us to do what it takes to restore health to the world's blue heart.

I share with Jean-Michel Cousteau the delight of being sprayed with whale breath at Stellwagen Bank, dodging sea turtles while looking for fossils of ice age animals at Gray's Reef off the coast of Georgia, of gliding among giant parrotfish in the Florida Keys, and immersing myself in a blizzard of eggs from spawning coral at the Flower Garden Banks off the coasts of Texas and Louisiana. There is haunting beauty and mystery in the protected shipwrecks lying within the Great Lakes, and others such as the remains of the Civil War vessel, *Monitor*, once a home for sailors, now a sanctuary for clouds of small fish and large grouper.

Those who visit any of California's four National Marine Sanctuaries have a chance to glimpse blue whales, the largest animals on earth, as well as some of the smallest, the minute planktonic creatures that drive ocean food webs. The Olympic National Marine Sanctuary holds healthy kelp forests adjacent to stands of ancient trees, and westward, in the Hawaiian Islands, special protection is being provided for some notable annual visitors, humpback whales. Coral reefs and the enormous diversity of life they contain are valued – and protected – in the Northwest Hawaiian Islands, American Samoa and a series of reefs, atolls and deep canyons near the Mariana Islands. These are all vital parts of the nation's treasury, places that give hope for the ocean, and therefore hope for ourselves.

I am pleased to be associated with the Ocean Futures Society, the organization Jean-Michel Cousteau founded to explore, communicate discoveries and messages to people and inspire them to take action to restore and protect the living ocean. They are making a difference – and so can you. Your reading of this book series is a strong first step in your understanding of the importance of protecting the sanctuaries for generations to come.

–Dr. Sylvia Earle
Oakland, California

Preface

The National Marine Sanctuary sites were designated in part because they were imperiled. Created more than 100 years after the national park system, these underwater treasures have been more difficult to explore and we have worked hard to learn their true value. By the time we did, we also discovered they were already at risk. Their very existence speaks to a reality that we now understand. It is clear they protect and promote the abundance and diversity of marine life essential to a healthy ocean. I am gratified that our leaders have seen the wisdom of placing a priority on protecting them now and for the future.

As the last book of the series was about to go to print, we were at a significant point in history, with the UN Climate Conference in Paris and IUCN's World Conservation Congress passing significant conservation and climate regulations. We have opened the Pandora's Box of what we thought was the cheap energy of petroleum and now, as a global community, we are seeing the urgent need to put a cap on carbon dioxide emissions to protect our resources, our future, and our water planet. We are finding cheap fuel is costing us too many lives, too much environmental degradation, and far too much impact on climate change. But how willing are we to protect the natural world on which we ultimately depend? The success of the Climate Conference might not be felt for years, but it is a turning point and I have much confidence we are turning in the right direction.

We live on a blue planet. The oceans cover over 70 percent of the surface of Earth. Their inhabitants supply over half of the oxygen we breathe, feed billions of people on the planet, and support our global economy through fisheries, tourism, and international trade, among countless more jobs that rely on the abundance of resources from the oceans. If we look at their value, simply in terms of money to our economy, the oceans are the world's seventh largest economy worth over $24 trillion dollars.

The oceans and its Sanctuaries will continue as emblems of how we proceed with our precious natural resources everywhere. The concept of Marine Protected Areas and Sanctuaries will expand and will re-seed and enliven vast areas of our imperiled seas.

The Pacific Islands are at the heart of climate change where sea level rise is significant. These special jewels in the Pacific are also a hot box of biodiversity with unique endemic species found nowhere else in the world. The protection of these special places today will ensure future generations will have the same privilege I have had in exploring these remote islands.

For now, enjoy the splendors in this book, realize what has been at risk, demand better than we now have, and then do everything you can to make it happen at every level.

This book shows you what is at stake. Dive in and explore your own National Marine Sanctuaries found around the Pacific Islands.

–Jean-Michel Cousteau
Santa Barbara, California

Introduction

About This Series

The four-book series, *Explore the National Marine Sanctuaries with Jean-Michel Cousteau*, has been developed in partnership with the National Marine Sanctuary system and Ocean Futures Society. Text in *italics* is excerpted from the previously-published (2007), limited-edition book *America's Underwater Treasures* by Jean-Michel Cousteau and Julie Robinson with photography by Carrie Vonderhaar. That book describes the experience and research of Jean-Michel and his Ocean Futures Team while diving all 13 underwater marine sanctuaries and the one underwater marine monument. Their experiences are captured in a film by the same name aired on PBS as part of *Jean-Michel Cousteau's Ocean Adventures*. The current series is offered to make information on these vital sanctuaries even more inclusive for the American public.

Each book in the series takes readers to one of the four regions of the country into which NOAA has organized its management of the National Marine Sanctuaries. This book, *Explore the Pacific Islands National Marine Sanctuaries with Jean-Michel Cousteau*, visits sanctuaries and a national monument off Hawai'i and American Samoa. The other books in the series are: *Explore the Southeast National Marine Sanctuaries with Jean-Michel Cousteau*, *Explore the West Coast National Marine Sanctuaries with Jean-Michel Cousteau* and *Explore the Northeast National Marine Sanctuaries with Jean-Michel Cousteau*.

Jean-Michel Cousteau.
Photo credit: Matthew Ferraro, Ocean Futures Society.

The first National Marine Sanctuary in the United States was established only three decades ago, while Yellowstone, the oldest of America's National Parks, was created in 1872. By comparison to parks, these natural marine jewels were damaged upon arrival. Only small portions remain pristine. For many, their designations arose amidst threats to one or a number of aspects to their survival. Like terrestrial parks, these are special habitats, managed zones for the recovery of critical species like humpback whales or juvenile rockfish but, most importantly, they attempt to preserve the integrity of the web of life.

Ironically, we discovered that managing these resources for sustainability was in truth an exercise in managing ourselves. And that's not, as we're still learning, an easy job. At each destination we were privileged witnesses to the real-time drama of marine conservation playing out across the United States. At the heart of it all, we found a powerful paradigm shift happening in environmentalism. Fishermen, environmentalists and scientists from opposite sides of the aisle were sitting down together with rolled-up sleeves, poring through scientific research, debating the merits of reserves and restoration, and coming to terms with this new definition of sanctuary. "These are," as Dan Basta, past director of the National Marine Sanctuary System, reminded us, "still works in progress."

About National Marine Sanctuaries

The Office of National Marine Sanctuaries, part of the National Oceanic and Atmospheric Administration, manages a national system of underwater-protected areas. The National Marine Sanctuary Act (created in 1972) authorizes the Secretary of Commerce to designate specific areas as National Marine Sanctuaries to promote comprehensive management of their special ecological, historical, recreational, and aesthetic resources. The Office of National Marine Sanctuaries currently manages thirteen National Marine Sanctuaries and one Marine National Monument established in areas where the natural or cultural resources are so significant that they warrant special status and protection.

On January 6, 2009, President George W. Bush established three additional marine national monuments, which were placed into the Pacific Reefs National Wildlife Refuge Complex. The three new marine national monuments are the Pacific Remote Islands Marine National Monument, Marianas Trench Marine National Monument, and the Rose Atoll Marine National Monument. Because Jean-Michel Cousteau and his Ocean Futures Society team have not yet dived in these three remote areas, they are not included in this series.

The Office of National Marine Sanctuaries works cooperatively with the public and federal, state, and local officials to promote conservation while allowing compatible commercial and recreational activities in the Sanctuaries. Increasing public awareness of our marine heritage, scientific research, monitoring, exploration, educational programs, and outreach are just a few of the ways the Office of National Marine Sanctuaries fulfills its mission to the American people. The primary objective of a sanctuary is to protect its natural and cultural features while allowing people to use and enjoy the ocean in a sustainable way. Sanctuary waters provide a secure habitat for species close to extinction and protect historically significant shipwrecks and artifacts. Sanctuaries serve as natural classrooms and laboratories for schoolchildren and researchers alike to promote understanding and stewardship of our oceans. They often are cherished recreational spots for sport fishing and diving and support commercial industries such as tourism, fishing and kelp harvesting.

Today (2007), only 0.01 percent of the world's oceans are effectively protected, a comparatively small measure, and one most scientists are quick to caution isn't a panacea for all the ocean's troubles. But it's enough nonetheless, to keep some fisheries managers and fishermen hopeful about sustainably harvesting fish from the sea. In the face of collapsing fisheries, "They may help some exploited species recover and keep others from going entirely extinct," according to Daniel Pauly, a researcher with the Fisheries Center at the University of British Columbia. He postulates that marine protected areas "should help prevent this, just like forests and other natural terrestrial habitats have enabled the survival of wildlife species, which agriculture would have otherwise rendered extinct."

The mission of NOAA's National Marine Sanctuaries is to serve as the trustee for the nation's system of marine protected areas, to conserve, protect, and enhance their biodiversity, ecological integrity and cultural legacy. The National Marine Sanctuary System consists of more than 150,000 square miles (390,000 km²) of marine and Great Lakes waters located from Washington State to the Florida Keys; from Lake Huron to American Samoa. Within these protected waters, giant humpback whales breed and calve their young, temperate reefs flourish, and shipwrecks tell stories of our maritime history. Today, our marine sanctuary system encompasses deep ocean gardens, nearshore coral reefs, whale migration corridors, deep sea canyons, and even underwater archeological sites. The sites range in size from the one-square-mile (2.6-square-kilometer) *Monitor* off North Carolina to more than 582,578 square miles (1,508,870 km²) in the Northwestern Hawaiian Islands, the largest marine protected areas in the world. Each sanctuary site is a unique place needing special protections. Natural classrooms, cherished recreational spots, and valuable commercial industries—marine sanctuaries represent many things to many people.

The National Marine Sanctuaries' Pacific Islands Region

The marine life found throughout the Insular Pacific Islands has shaped the way of life for this region for thousands of years. For most people, the Pacific Islands conjure up visions of palm trees, beautiful beaches and a variety of ocean activities. But there is another world beneath the waves where amazing creatures swim through tropical waters that range from abyssal deeps to shallow, stunning coral reefs.

Two ocean areas in Hawai'i and one in American Samoa have been set aside to help preserve the region's special natural and cultural heritage. NOAA's Office of National Marine Sanctuaries Pacific Islands Region manages these marine protected areas in partnership with the State of Hawai'i (Department of Land and Natural Resources) and the Territory of American Samoa Department of Commerce.

This book will introduce readers to the **Hawaiian Islands Humpback Whale National Marine Sanctuary,** the **National Marine Sanctuary of American Samoa** and **Papahānaumokuākea Marine National Monument**.

Pacific Islands Region Sanctuary Offices:
726 South Kīhei Road
Kīhei, Maui, Hawai'i 96753
Telephone: 808-879-2818

6600 Kalanian'ole Highway, Suite 302
Honolulu, Hawai'i 96825
Telephone: 808-397-2404

Note: All of the Humpback Whale images photographed by Carrie Vonderhaar were photographed under the authority of NMFS Permit No. 642-1536-01 issued under the authority of the Marine Mammal Protection Act and Endangered Species Act.

Hawaiian Islands Humpback Whale National Marine Sanctuary

About the Hawaiian Islands
Humpback Whale National Marine Sanctuary

Hawaiian Islands Humpback Whale National Marine Sanctuary, which is jointly managed by the National Oceanic and Atmospheric Administration and the State of Hawai'i, lies within the shallow warm waters surrounding the main Hawaiian Islands and constitutes one of the world's most important humpback whale habitats. Through education, research and resource protection activities, the sanctuary strives to protect humpback whales and their habitat in Hawai'i. The sanctuary is located from the shoreline to a depth of 100 fathoms (600 feet/183 km depth) in the four island area of Maui; Penguin Bank; and off the north shore of Kaua'i, the north and south shores of O'ahu, and the north Kona and Kohala coasts of the Big Island.

A humpback whale calf breaches in front of the island of Maui, Hawaii.
Photo credit: Carrie Vonderhaar, Ocean Futures Society.

The Big Island of Hawai'i is actually the highest mountain on the planet when measured from its base on the ocean floor to its terrestrial peak. Magma pushing up through the sea from deep within the Earth's crust has progressively formed these basalt peaks over five to seventy million years. These islands are also the farthest from any point of land and over time, thousands of species have arrived here, carried by wings or the sea. More than 25 percent of Hawai'i's reef organisms are endemic, living only here. Endangered monk seals, threatened green sea turtles, manta rays, and tiger sharks swim in these waters. But it is the Pacific humpback whale for which the Hawaiian Islands Humpback Whale National Marine Sanctuary was originally designated.

Humpback whales in singing position.
Photo credit: HIHWNMS/NOAA Fisheries Permit #782-1719

Beginning in late fall and early winter, humpbacks begin arriving in the Hawaiian Islands from their summer feeding grounds in British Columbia and Alaska. Scientists cannot say for certain why the whales embark on the annual journey away from their feeding grounds, fasting for months and expending significant energy on a journey of thousands of miles—among the longest of any migrations in the animal kingdom. All that is clear is that the Hawaiian Islands are somehow inextricably linked to the whales' cycle of life.

Why a National Marine Sanctuary?

Humpback whales were once plentiful in oceans worldwide. The global population of humpbacks was depleted by the commercial whaling industry at the start of the 20th century. In 1973, with the passing of the Endangered Species Act, the United States government made it illegal to hunt, harm, or disturb humpback whales. The humpback whale has been listed as a federally endangered species since 1973. A variety of laws protect these animals, including the Marine Mammal Protection Act, the Endangered Species Act, state wildlife laws, and the National Marine Sanctuaries Act. In addition, they are protected as a resource of national significance within Hawaiian Islands Humpback Whale National Marine Sanctuary.

No one knows exactly when humpback whales first began wintering in the warm, shallow waters around the Hawaiian Islands. Narrative reports from whalers document the appearance of these majestic giants in Hawai'i in the 1840s, but little evidence substantiates an earlier presence. But arrive they did, and today, the waters around the main Hawaiian Islands constitute one of the world's most important North Pacific humpback whale habitats, and the only place in U.S. coastal waters where humpbacks reproduce.

A humpback whale cow, calf and male escort under water.
Photo credit: Carrie Vonderhaar, Ocean Futures Society.

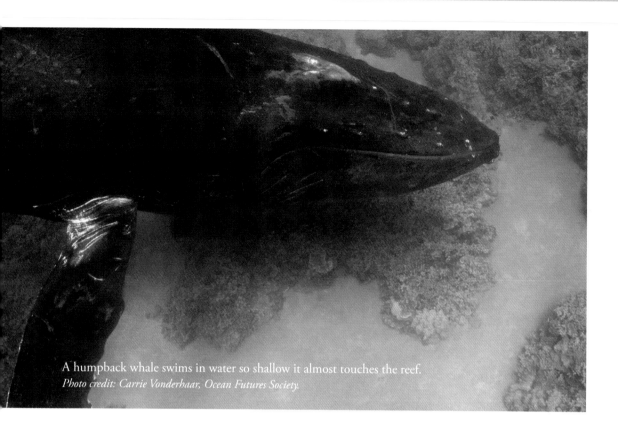

A humpback whale swims in water so shallow it almost touches the reef.
Photo credit: Carrie Vonderhaar, Ocean Futures Society.

In March 1982, the National Oceanic and Atmospheric Administration stated that certain areas around the Hawaiian Islands should become a national marine sanctuary. Public workshops were held to allow scientists and the community to discuss the purpose of such a sanctuary and to evaluate the issues related to the management of a sanctuary. Soon after, some members of the community voiced opposition, fearing that a marine sanctuary would bring additional restrictions on fishing and vessel traffic. In response to these concerns, Hawai'i's then Governor Ariyoshi suspended further consideration of the site in early 1984.

Six years later, in October 1990, President George H.W. Bush directed the Secretary of Defense to immediately discontinue the use of Kahoʻolawe as a weapons range. Congress once again directed NOAA to determine the feasibility of establishing a national marine sanctuary in the waters around the island and elsewhere in Hawai'i.

Congress, in consultation with the State of Hawai'i, designated the Hawaiian Islands Humpback Whale National Marine Sanctuary on November 4, 1992. The waters surrounding the Hawaiian Islands are essential breeding, calving and nursing areas for the North Pacific humpback whale. Protection of this important ecological habitat is necessary for the long-term recovery of the whale population. The Hawaiian Islands National Marine Sanctuary Act identified the following purposes for the sanctuary: to protect humpback whales and their habitat within the sanctuary; to educate and interpret for the public the relationship of humpback whales and the Hawaiian Islands marine environment; to manage human uses of the sanctuary consistent with the Hawaiian Islands National Marine Sanctuary Act and the National Marine Sanctuaries Act; and to identify marine resources and ecosystems of national significance for possible inclusion in the sanctuary.

A spectacular breaching humpback whale.
Photo credit: HIHWNMS/NOAA Fisheries Permit #782-1438.

13

Humpback whales are not the only animals to mate in the Hawaiian waters. Here, Ocean Futures diver Matthew Ferraro observes the courting dance of endangered green sea turtles.
Photo credit: Carrie Vonderhaar, Ocean Futures Society

The public, though still divided in its support, was assured that the sanctuary essentially would incorporate existing restrictions to enhance the protection of humpback whales and their habitat. Those restrictions primarily dealt with approaching and harassment of the whale population, discharge of wastes into the water, and alteration of the sea bed. On June 5, 1997, over four years after the Hawaiian Islands Humpback Whale National Marine Sanctuary was designated the nation's 12th marine sanctuary, Hawai'i Governor Benjamin Cayetano formally approved of the sanctuary in state waters.

Resources Within the Hawaiian Islands Humpback Whale National Marine Sanctuary

CULTURAL RESOURCES

Hawai'i has a long and continuous history of coastal and marine activity. Maritime cultural landscapes are areas possessing resources that reflect these past and current human uses. For instance, the many Hawaiian fishponds and fish traps along the coast make up an aquaculture landscape. Inter-island steamship wrecks and historic landings contribute to a plantation-era landscape. The many navy shipwrecks and sunken aircraft make up a military landscape underwater. Maritime landscapes reflect historic eras (pre and post Western contact), major events and critical activities, and provide a better context for understanding the actual heritage resources within the sanctuary.

A Corsair fighting plane off Honolulu. *Photo credit: Carrie Vonderhaar, Ocean Futures Society.*

Following Polynesian settlement, advanced aquaculture techniques flourished in the Hawaiian Islands, where there may have been between 400 and 500 stone fish ponds, producing something around two million pounds (900,000 kg) of fish annually. Today only a handful of ponds are in condition to produce some fish. Such stone remains can sometimes endure hundreds of years in relatively good shape. In 1997, University of Hawai'i maritime archaeology students mapped the stone fish traps at Kaloko-Honokōhau National Park on the Island of Hawai'i. The sanctuary has also supported efforts to rebuild the fish pond adjacent to its Maui headquarters. Bishop Museum's inventory of coastal fishponds records the location of at least 60 structures within the sanctuary.

Fish trap structures at Kaloko-Honokōhau National Historic Park.   *Photo credit: Hans Van Tilburg/NOAA.*

Shell fishing hooks, as well as scattered basalt artifacts, stone octopus lure weights, fish trap weights and canoe anchors, can be found on certain nearshore reefs within the sanctuary. A 1996 University of Hawai'i survey focused on one such site, a scattered collection of stone artifacts, sinkers and octopus lures, directly off the Waikiki shoreline.

The wreck site of the brig *Cleopatra's Barge* highlights the interactions between Native Hawaiians and foreign cultures in the decades following Western contact. The luxurious vessel, built by George Crowninshield of New England in 1816, was sold to King Kamehameha II (Liholiho) in 1820 and renamed *Ha'aheo o Hawai'i* (*Pride of Hawai'i*), to serve as the royal yacht. Lost in 1824 in Hanalei Bay, the remains of *Ha'aheo o Hawai'i* were excavated by Dr. Paul Johnston of the Smithsonian Institute. A great variety of Native Hawaiian, Asian and Western artifacts currently await return to proper curatorial facilities in Hawai'i, telling the story of social and economic change among the Islands.

An 1818 painting of *Cleopatra's Barge* by George Ropes. *Image credit: Wikimedia commons.*

The historic importance of the Hawaiian Islands to Western whaling ships has been well-documented. Soon after the *Balaena* and the *Equator* harpooned the first whale off Kealakekua Bay in 1819, Hawai'i won its place on the maps of the whalers. As Pacific whaling grounds became dominated by American vessels in the mid-19th century, whale oil became a major economic component of economic expansion in both New England and the Hawaiian Islands. Some residents in Hawai'i today can trace their lineage to the frequent deserter from a whaling ship. There are at least 18 documented wrecks of whalers in and around the Hawaiian island chain, five of these being located within the sanctuary. The whalers *Drymo* (1845), *Paulina* (1860), and *Young Hero* (1858) lost near Maui, the *Jefferson* (1842) in Hanalei Bay on Kaua'i, and the *Helvetius* (1834) near O'ahu, testify to the once active American involvement in Pacific whale hunting. Fortunately, the remains of this brutal activity now lie within the sanctuary which now features conservation rather than exploitation.

Navy fuel tanker shipwreck, Shipwreck Beach, Lānaʻi, Hawaiʻi.
Photo credit: Steve L. Martin.

The sanctuary's boundaries also include "Shipwreck Beach" on the north shore of Lānaʻi Island. During the 19th and early 20th centuries the U.S. Navy and inter-island navigation companies used Shipwreck Beach as an area for the intentional abandonment of vessels, a "rotten row" of old ships. Many vessels were also lost on the coast's treacherous reefs by accident. Several of these now historic sites have been surveyed, such as the Pearl Harbor survivor *YO-21,* the schooner *Mary Alice,* and the Hawaiian steamship SS *Hornet,* but many other wrecks along the eight-mile stretch have yet to be identified. Shipwreck Beach is also a location of a Hawaiian battleground. Seeking to strike against the political satellite of Maui, Kalaniopuʻu, a war chief from the Island of Hawaiʻi, landed his warriors along the north shore and raided Lānaʻi in 1778.

Unprecedented naval activity took place among the Hawaiian Islands during World War II, in the skies as well as on and under the sea. Hundreds of navy fighter aircraft and pilots took part in intensive training activities in preparation for combat operations in the Pacific. There are over 1,500 naval aircraft sunk in the vicinity of the Hawaiian Islands, and of these some 39 are known to have been lost in sanctuary waters. Some of these submerged aircraft crash sites are war graves. These protected resources, property of the federal government, bear witness to our nation's commitment and sacrifice during the war, a period which changed the shape of the entire Pacific region.

Shipwreck and aircraft sites within the sanctuary also function as sport diving destinations, wreck sites enjoyed by local and visiting divers. The steamship SS *Maui* lost on the Island of Hawai'i, the F4U-1 Corsair in O'ahu's Maunalua Bay, the PB4Y-1 Liberator near Maui, numerous U.S. Navy landing craft lost during training operations on beaches throughout the main Hawaiian Islands, and now the *Carthaginian II,* the replica whaling supply brig which once welcomed Lahaina visitors to tour on board, now entice divers to share in a bit of the maritime past. The sport diving industry plays an important role in sharing Hawai'i's connection to the sea.

Ocean Futures diver Matthew Ferraro at the "artificial reef" wreck "Corsair", a former fighting plane.
Photo credit: Carrie Vonderhaar, Ocean Futures Society.

The Hokule'a, an ancient Polynesian voyaging vessel, is most likely the type of craft that the first Polynesians used to discover the Hawaiian Islands. *Photo credit: Tom Ordway, Ocean Futures Society.*

Heritage resources within the sanctuary reflect the broad historic phases of past maritime activity: Native Hawaiian aquaculture and fishing, Pacific whaling, inter-island sail and steam navigation, and naval activity among the islands. Many of the maritime heritage resources within the sanctuary fall within state waters. The state agency for preservation management of these heritage resources is the State Historic Preservation Office under the Department of Land and Natural Resources.

Key Species Within the Sanctuary

HUMPBACK WHALES

Humpback whales may live for 40-50 years, reaching a length of about 45 feet (14 meters), and a weight of 45-50 tons (41-45 metric tons). They become sexually mature at about 5-9 years of age. The gestation period for a humpback whale is 10-12 months. These whales are recognized by their long, white pectoral (side) flippers. The under-side of the tail flukes has white patterns that are unique to individual whales and are used by researchers to identify individual animals.

Each fluke of a humpback whale is as distinctive as a human fingerprint.
Photo credit: Carrie Vonderhaar, Ocean Futures Society.

The humpback whale is an endangered species. Scientists estimate that the pre-whaling population of the North Pacific stock of humpback whales numbered approximately 15,000. In 1993 it was estimated that there were 6,000 whales in the North Pacific Ocean, and that 4,000 of those came to Hawai'i. The population is estimated to be growing at between 4% and 7% per year. Today, as many as 12,000 humpback whales may visit Hawai'i each year.

Most of the North Pacific stock of humpback whales winter in three nearshore lower latitude mating and calving areas: Hawai'i, western Mexico and the islands of southern Japan. During the spring and summer they migrate as much as 3,000 miles (4,800 km) to feeding areas over the continental shelf of the Pacific Rim, from the coast of California north to the Bering Sea (between Alaska and Siberia). Humpbacks continuously travel at approximately three to seven miles per hour (5-11 km/hr) with very few stops. The main Hawaiian Islands may contain the largest seasonal population of North Pacific humpbacks in the world.

Two humpbacks swim close to Fabien and Céline Cousteau, who are snorkeling near shore.
Photo credit: Carrie Vonderhaar, Ocean Futures Society.

The upper jaw of a feeding humpback whale. The inside of the baleen plates are hairy, allowing the whale to trap tiny food particles in its mouth. *Photo credit: NOAA.*

The North Pacific stock of humpback whales feed during the summer in northern waters (between approximate latitudes of 40-75° N). The cool, nutrient rich waters around Alaska provide ideal feeding locations. Humpback whales have plate-like bristles known as baleen in their mouth instead of teeth. They feed on krill and small schooling fishes, such as capelin and herring. A variety of feeding methods are used including bubble net feeding and lunge feeding. Humpbacks rarely feed in their wintering areas and it is not known if they feed along their migratory routes.

Hawai'i is the only state in the United States where humpback whales mate, calve, and nurse their young. Humpbacks may find Hawai'i suitable because of the warm waters, the underwater visibility, the variety of ocean depths, and the lack of natural predators. Mothers can be seen breaching alongside their calves and males can be seen competing with one another for females in fierce battles.

A humpback whale mother and calf.
Photo credit: Carrie Vonderhaar, Ocean Futures Society.

Many secrets of the elusive humpbacks are still hidden from the eyes of their keen observers. Mating, for instance, has never been observed in forty years of study. These whales, unlike their libidinous cetacean cousins, prefer more discrete affairs. So scientists journey to Maui and the channels between Lānaʻi, Kahoʻolawe and Molokaʻi, where by February the sea is crowded with whales. Every age and sex class can be accounted for and the groupings of whales take distinctive patterns. Newborn calves are protectively shielded beneath their mother's "chins," enveloped within the wings of their giant pectoral fins. Mother and baby are often found in the company of an escort, usually a young adult male. Escorts may stay with mother-calf pairs for hours or days, possibly a form of gentle courtship that precedes mating. These pairings also seem to protect mother whales from harassment by other males in the midst of fierce competitions for mating that are being waged all around.

Although many species of whales and dolphins are vocal, humpback whales are the whales best known for their songs. The "humpback song" consists of sequences of sounds that are repeated over and over in a pattern. Patterns of humpback whale sounds change from year to year and can vary in different parts of the ocean. Scientists have found that male humpback whales sing while in their breeding grounds. Other humpback whale sounds have also been recorded in feeding areas. Each of the sounds made by the humpback is thought to have a distinct purpose. Research continues on this fascinating topic.

"Often you'll hear folks comment on the humpback's "vocalizations," but the truth of the matter is that whales don't have vocal chords. What they do have are valves and sacs in their respiratory system that generate amazingly powerful sound. It's so powerful that when you're in the water with a singer, every air cavity in your body is assaulted by the vibrations. You have to remember that these sounds are coming from a 50-ton (45-metric ton) beast." [Gary Holland, Sound Engineer, Ocean Futures Society]

Mother-calf pair with an escort whale.
Photo credit: Carrie Vonderhaar, Ocean Futures Society.

Suspended in liquid blue, Fabien Cousteau free-dives near an adult humpback. "The core of your body vibrates with the songs of other humpback whales in the distance…from the tips of your fins all the way up through your body. It's awe-inspiring."
Photo credit: Carrie Vonderhaar, Ocean Futures Society.

When a 40-ton (36-metric ton) whale completely clears the water and crashes back into the sea, a thunderous splash sends an acoustic message that this is one powerful whale likely to impart good genes to his progeny.

Breaching is display behavior and humpbacks will propel their bodies almost entirely out of the water, creating a huge splash on landing. *Photo credit: Carrie Vonderhaar, Ocean Futures Society.*

Humpback whale populations are still relatively unknown. In an effort to provide a relative approximation of humpback whale numbers and distribution patterns locally over the years and to raise awareness of the species, the sanctuary sponsors community events such as the Sanctuary Ocean Count.[1]

The Sanctuary Ocean Count was initiated as a means to provide Hawai'i residents and visitors with the opportunity to observe humpback whales in their breeding grounds by conducting a yearly shore-based census during the peak breeding season. Although the census does not claim to provide scientifically accurate results, it serves as a tool to supplement scientific information gathered from other research activities. The count also provides some information on how whales use in-shore waters on an average peak season day. The Sanctuary Ocean Count serves to promote public awareness about humpback whales, the sanctuary, and shore-based whale watching opportunities.

1   http://hawaiihumpbackwhale.noaa.gov/involved/ocprojectinfo.html

Each year, the Hawaiian Islands Humpback Whale National Marine Sanctuary hosts the Sanctuary Ocean Count. This is a fun volunteer activity for residents and visitors on the islands, and it helps to provide information on humpback whales around the Hawaiian Islands. *Photo credit: NOAA.*

The Sanctuary Ocean Count is held concurrently on Oʻahu, Kauaʻi, the Big Island, and, when funding allows, on Kahoʻolawe. Volunteers assisting with the project spend their morning counting whales and recording their behaviors. To date, the Sanctuary Ocean Count covers 60 sites on four islands, with an enlistment of over 2,000 volunteers. In the future, the sanctuary hopes to expand this project to other islands. The Sanctuary Ocean Count provides Hawaiʻi residents and visitors with the opportunity to actively participate in evaluating the status of humpback whales. The count is held the last Saturday of January, February and March of each year from 8:00 a.m. to 12:15 p.m.

HAWAIʻI'S STATE FISH

In 1984, the Picasso triggerfish was named as Hawaiʻi's official state fish. Its Hawaiian name, humuhumunukunukuapuaʻa, means "nose like a pig." In fact, triggerfishes are known to grunt like pigs if they are unkindly pulled out of the water. They can swim backwards and forwards. Their common name comes from the arrangement of their two dorsal spines: The larger spine can be locked or released by the smaller one (the trigger). This spine-locking mechanism allows triggerfishes to lodge themselves firmly in crevices where predators cannot harm or remove them.

Picasso triggerfish. *Photo credit: Dr. Richard C. Murphy, Ocean Futures Society.*

Pacific golden plover in March. *Photo credit: Noah Kahn/US Fish and Wildlife Service.*

PACIFIC GOLDEN PLOVER

Every year, kolea (Hawaiian name for Pacific golden plover) embark on an amazing journey flying south from Alaska to places like Hawai'i. They fly up to 3,500 miles (5,600 km) non-stop. In Alaska, they breed and nest in diverse habitats, such as tundra, while feeding on insects and worms. They begin their migration to warmer weather around August, with adults arriving first, followed by juveniles. In Hawai'i, kolea may be seen on rooftops or feeding in grassy areas. Beginning in late February, kolea molt and their golden winter plumage is replaced by darker summer breeding colors.

Emerging Environmental Issues

ENTANGLEMENT

Entanglement in marine debris, such as fishing gear, is a growing problem for marine mammals. It can hinder diving, swimming, feeding, and surfacing activities, as well as the overall behavior of the animal. Entanglement threatens humpback whales and many other marine animals. The sources of these entanglements are extensive and diverse.

Marine mammal entanglement, or by-catch, is a global problem that every year results in the death of hundreds of thousands of whales, dolphins, porpoises and seals. Entanglement may result in starvation or drowning due to restricted movement, physical trauma and systemic infections, and/or contribute to other threats, like ship strikes. For Hawai'i's smaller marine mammals, such as monk seals and dolphins, death is typically immediate and caused by drowning. However, large whales, like the humpback whale, can typically pull gear, or parts of it, off the ocean floor, and are generally not in immediate risk of drowning.

Humpback whale entangled in fishing gear off Hawai'i in 2006.
Photo credit: NOAA.

However, marine mammal entanglements in Hawai'i have been documented for decades and they pose a significant threat to the North Pacific stock of humpback whales which migrate to Hawai'i each winter. A portion of these animals get entangled in marine debris in their feeding grounds in the northern Pacific and carry it with them to Hawai'i, while others get entangled in the breeding grounds. Entanglement in fishing gear and other marine debris may result in drowning, starvation, physical trauma, systemic infections, or increased susceptibility to other threats, such as ship strikes.

Some of these animals free themselves from the entangling gear, as indicated by the scars and wounds that the gear has left behind. The documentation and monitoring of these scars has suggested that in some regions of the North Pacific as many as 78% of the humpback whales have been entangled recently. Overall, scientists still do not know how many whales die each year from this threat.

Cutting free a 45-foot (14-meter), 40-ton (36-metric ton), typically free-swimming animal is not an easy task, and can be quite dangerous for humans and the animal alike. The Hawaiian Islands Entanglement Response Network is a community-based network, led by the Hawaiian Islands Humpback Whale National Marine Sanctuary. Network partners include NOAA's Pacific Islands Regional Office, Hawai'i's Department of Land and Natural Resources, the United States Coast Guard, whale researchers, Hawai'i's tour industry, and many private organizations and individuals. The Network's response efforts are authorized under NOAA Fisheries' Marine Mammal Health and Stranding Response Program. The Network has grown since its inception in 2002 and now comprises over 230 participants who have received various levels of training in order to support large whale response efforts statewide.

Healed wounds along a whale's back.
Photo credit: Richard Lundholm.

As of May, 2012:

- Over 211 whales had been reported entangled; 112 of these reports were con-firmed to be large whale entanglements.

- More than 120 on-water responses had been mounted (some reports could not be responded to because of time of day, weather, and/or remoteness).

- Sixteen whales were freed of entangling gear, with over 6,700 feet (2,000 meters) of line removed.

- Recovered gear has been identified as marine debris, mooring gear, local fish-ing gear, and fishing gear set far from Hawai'i. Gear has been traced back to the Pribilof Islands, the Aleutians, and Southeast Alaska—in some cases the source of the entanglement was more than a 2,450 nautical mile (2,800 miles/4,500 km) straightline distance from Hawai'i.

Rescuers position themselves to remove entangled gear from a humpback whale off Hawai'i.
Photo credit: NOAA.

VESSEL COLLISIONS

Collision with vessels is recognized as a source of injury and death for endangered humpback whales in Hawai'i. In recent years, the occurrence of vessel collisions with humpback whales in Hawai'i has increased. NOAA has confirmed 38 vessel strikes in Hawaiian waters from 1975 to 2007. Seven of those 38 ship strikes occurred during the 2006 whale season and six occurred during the 2007 whale season.

The smaller humpback has major injuries which are the result of being struck by a vessel.
Photo Credit: HIHWNMS/NOAA Fisheries Permit #782-1719.

Due to the level of complexity and danger involved no person should ever attempt to disentangle a marine mammal on their own or without proper authorization. Instead, immediately contact NOAA Fisheries at 1-888-256-9840 or contact the United States Coast Guard on VHF channel 16 (156.8 Mhz).

ACOUSTIC IMPACTS

Acoustic impacts are not clearly understood, but human-caused underwater noise could potentially adversely affect humpback whales by disrupting resting, feeding, courtship, calving, nursing, migration or other activities. Researchers suggest that increased background noise and specific sound sources might impact marine animals in several ways. The effects vary depending upon the intensity and frequency of the sound, and other variables. Potential impacts include sounds that cause marine animals to alter their behavior; prevent marine animals from hearing important sounds (masking); or cause hearing loss (temporary or permanent) or tissue damage in marine animals. The sanctuary currently plays a supporting role through collaborative research activities which have measured levels of sound from coastal construction, demolition and typical vessel noise.

By the first days of February, the team was on the water from dawn to dusk observing, diving and filming the humpbacks with Scott's[2] expert help. Filming or even being in the water near these endangered species must be conducted under a federal permit and with the supervision of a cetacean biologist. Scott had his hands full with the difficult task of being both a hall monitor and teacher in an ocean classroom. For divers, the sheer size, presence and noise of whales under water can be disorienting. And like all wild animals, even these giant leviathans have established rules of interaction and an invisible border of personal space. But with Scott's coaching, we quickly had mastered humpback etiquette and the whales seemed more willing then to allow us to film in their presence.

---

2   Scott Spitz, PhD—marine mammal biologist

Humpback whales rest under water.
Photo credit: Credit: Carrie Vonderhaar, Ocean Futures Society.

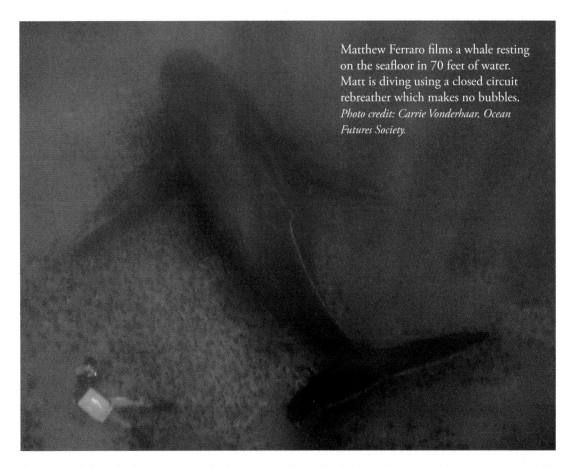

Matthew Ferraro films a whale resting on the seafloor in 70 feet of water. Matt is diving using a closed circuit rebreather which makes no bubbles.
Photo credit: Carrie Vonderhaar, Ocean Futures Society.

Scott explained why in general whales don't like bubbles: they can be associated with the threat postures male humpbacks use to deter other males. They also make a heck of a lot of noise, probably an unpleasant sound to these acoustically sensitive animals. For filming purposes, open-circuit scuba was ruled out. Matt and Yves[3] would film with the aid of the Inspiration rebreathers. But Carrie[4] learned at the last minute she would have to free-dive: the team had to minimize the impact of too many divers in the water at the same time. By the end of the expedition, every whale image she captured was on a breathhold dive.

---

3   Matt Ferraro, Cinematographer, and Yves Lefevre, Cinematographer, Ocean Futures Society.
4   Carrie Vonderhaar, Chief Expedition Photographer, Ocean Futures Society.

OPEN OCEAN AQUACULTURE

Humpback whales prefer calm, relatively shallow waters, located just off the leeward sides of the main Hawaiian Islands. These areas may also be desirable for open ocean aquaculture projects. Aquaculture structures may be large, suspended in the water column, and moored to the ocean bottom, although new designs that are currently being developed include unmoored structures that float in the water column. Potential concerns for humpback whales and other marine species may include loss of habitat and entanglement. Additional investigation and monitoring is required for other potential impacts of concern. The Hawaiian Islands Humpback Whale National Marine Sanctuary and the University of Hawai'i are engaging cultural and fishpond practitioners, community members, farmers, business representatives, subject matter experts, state and federal agency representatives and marine resource managers to discuss and learn more about this emerging issue.

University of Hawai'i's SeaStation 3000 aquaculture cage, approximately 40 feet below the surface offshore of Honolulu.
Photo credit: NOAA.

Research Within the Sanctuary

The sanctuary's science and research program focuses on two of the most significant threats to humpback whales—entanglements and vessel collisions—as well as other human activities. Sanctuary science and research staff collaborate with a variety of partners locally, nationally and internationally to understand the scope and impact of these threats to humpback whales throughout their range in the North Pacific.

- **SPLASH:** Sanctuary scientists coordinated the largest whale research project ever completed. The Structure of Population, Levels of Abundance, and Status of Humpbacks (SPLASH) project, composed of over 400 researchers, 50 organizations and 10 countries, generated the most accurate population estimates ever calculated for humpback whales in Hawai'i and the North Pacific. The 2006 SPLASH results found the Hawaiian humpback whale population to be approximately 10,000 whales with an annual growth rate of six percent. The project also studied the known key threats to humpback whales (entanglement and vessel-whale collisions) and some other threats (pollution) throughout their entire habitat—something that had never been done before for any whale species—and found that entanglement in fishing gear and debris is at epidemic levels in the North Pacific.

Research Assets

KOHOLĀ

This new (2012) 36-foot (11-meter) vessel was specifically built and customized for large whale response, disentanglement and research for the Hawaiian Islands Humpback Whale National Marine Sanctuary. Based in the heart of the sanctuary, the vessel's homeport will be primarily in Maui at Ma'alaea Harbor near the sanctuary's Kīhei facilities. The boat's features include:
- True turn-key response boat ready to respond immediately.
- Built-in storage for 15-foot (4.5-meter) rapid deployment inflatable.
- Davit for lifting heavy equipment.
- Custom-designed upper helm station provides the boat operator with excellent visibility for safe operation around whales.

The Koholā is used by the Hawaiian Islands Humpback Whale National Marine Sanctuary for large whale research and disentanglement efforts. *Photo credit: NOAA.*

- Multiple stations for observers.
- Versatile platform for tagging, observation, health assessment and response to marine mammals in distress.
- Support for research and monitoring of fish, corals and maritime heritage resources through dive operations by cooperating partners.

Visiting the Sanctuary

Note: In the last section of the book, "When You Visit the Sanctuaries," is detailed information about resources found within each sanctuary to help visitors have an enjoyable and productive visit.

VISITOR'S CENTER

Maui Office and Visitor Center
726 South Kīhei Road
Kīhei, HI 96753

Open Monday - Friday
10 a.m. - 3 p.m.
Admission is free

The beachfront setting of the sanctuary facility in Kīhei, Maui, offers both scenic beauty and ecological significance. Visitors to the site will discover a living classroom, with many opportunities to enjoy the simple pleasures of nature watching. During winter, koholā (humpback whales) are seen on the horizon with frequent activity close to shore. The deck of the main building provides a viewscope for observing the ever-changing scene along Maui's coastline.

Inside the Visitor Center, exhibits and artifacts highlight the significance of humpback whales from the perspectives of both science and culture. Open during weekdays, the center offers information for adults and children and a corps of dedicated volunteers, well-versed in whale facts and legends, will share their knowledge. Education materials and special programs are available. The stone walls of Koʻieʻie, an intricately constructed fishpond, are a record of the kinship that Native Hawaiians had with the sea when they inhabited the area long ago.

The 4,600 square-foot (427-square meter) single story Sanctuary Learning Center is located next to the Sanctuary Visitor Center. The building provides facilities for offices and classroom space for school groups and public programs. The facility will also enhance interaction with

Hawaiian Islands Humpback Whale National Marine Sanctuary Visitor Center. *Photo credit: NOAA/HIHWNMS.*

the greater Pacific and international marine mammal management community. The $6.5 million building broke ground in 2004, and construction was completed in 2009.

In an effort to green operations and reduce costs, 186 solar panels were installed on the roofs of the building located at the sanctuary's Kīhei campus. The goal of the 42-kilowatt array of photovoltaic panels is to produce enough electricity from the sun to eliminate having to use energy from the grid that is produced from burning oil. Up to $25,000 a year is being saved in electricity costs. Other energy conservation measures of the renovated historic building originally built in 1941 include a weather sealed exterior, insulation, more efficient air conditioning system, instant hot water heater, efficient lighting with occupancy sensors, solar powered parking lighting and more.

Photovoltaic cells on the roof of the Sanctuary Learning Center. *Photo credit: NOAA/HIHWNMS.*

O'ahu Headquarters Office
6600 Kalaniana'ole Highway, Suite 301
Honolulu, HI 96825
Phone: (808) 397-2651 or toll free 1-888-55-WHALE

The Honolulu office of the sanctuary houses many of the sanctuary's administrative staff, including the sanctuary superintendent. The office serves as the base of operations for the Sanctuary Ocean Count project and also serves as a venue for scheduled volunteer training, workshops, and meetings. Education and outreach materials are available.

Kaua'i Office
Kukui Grove Executive Center
4370 Kukui Grove Street, Suite 206
Lihu'e, HI 96766
Phone: (808) 246-2860

The sanctuary office in Lihuʻe, Kauaʻi, is a small office in a commercial office complex that serves as the base of operations for sanctuary programs on Kauaʻi. The office also serves as a venue for scheduled volunteer training, workshops, and meetings. Education and outreach materials are available. People are asked to call ahead to schedule a visit as staff are not always on site.

Kona Office
73-4460 Queen Kaʻahumanu Highway, Suite 112
Kailua-Kona, HI 96740
Phone: (808) 327-3697

The sanctuary office in Kona, is a small office located at the Natural Energy Lab Hawaiʻi Authority that serves as the base of operations for sanctuary programs on the Big Island. People are asked to call ahead to schedule a visit as staff are not always on site.

State Office
Department of Land and Natural Resources
1151 Punchbowl Street, #330
Honolulu, HI 96813
Phone: (808) 587-0106

The state sanctuary office is located within the State of Hawaiʻi Department of Land and Natural Resources in Honolulu.

ECOTOURISM/WHALE WATCHING
Humpback whales visit Hawaiian waters each year from November to May with the peak of the season being from January to March. There are a variety of ways in which to catch a glimpse of Hawaiʻi's humpback whales. Boat tours and whale watching cruises have become increasingly popular. In Hawaiʻi, Maui is a top whale watching spot for boat-based viewing; however, whale watching cruises are available at most harbors around the state.

Guidelines for Wildlife Protection and Human Safety

All ocean users (power boaters, sailors, jet skiers, kayakers, paddlers, windsurfers, swimmers, divers, etc.) must:

- **Keep a Safe Distance** – Please do not chase, closely approach, surround, swim with, or attempt to feed or touch marine wildlife.
- Follow federal regulations that prohibit approaching whales (by any means) within 100 yards (90 m) when on or in the water, and 1,000 feet (300 m) when operating an aircraft. **These regulations apply to all ocean users throughout the Hawaiian Islands.**
- For Hawaiian monk seals and other species of whales and dolphins the **recommended distance for observation** is 50 yards (45m) when on the beaches or on the water and 1,000 feet (300m) when operating an aircraft.
- Use extra caution **in the vicinity of mothers and young** and in other sensitive wildlife habitat such as feeding, nursing, or resting areas.
- For **sea turtles**, please remember that feeding, touching, or attempting to ride them can cause distress. Please observe from a distance and allow them a clear escape route to deeper water. Never entice marine wildlife to approach you.
- When **on or under the water**, please remember that the Hawaiian Islands Humpback Whale National Marine Sanctuary is there to protect humpback whales. Disturbing the whales can disrupt vital calving, nursing, and breeding behaviors.

Whales can be seen quite easily from most shorelines around the Hawaiian Islands. People can take a trip to the beach or a scenic lookout and watch for the blows, pectoral flipper slaps, fluke-up dives, and breaches[5] of Hawai'i's humpbacks. The sanctuary's top ten viewing locations are: (O'ahu) Makapu'u Lighthouse, Halona Blowhole, Hanauma Bay, Diamond Head Scenic Lookout; (Maui) Papawai Point, Sanctuary Education Center;

5   http://hawaiihumpbackwhale.noaa.gov/explore/humpback_whale.html#behavior

(Hawai'i) Lapakahi State Historical Park, Kapa'a Beach Park and (Kaua'i) Kilauea Point National Wildlife Refuge. Drivers are cautioned to be safe when whale watching—they should always pull off the road to view whales, and should never stop or slow down in the road to take photos.

BOATING

All boat operators in the sanctuary need to be aware of rules and guidelines that are in place to help protect humpback whales:

- **Keep a Sharp Lookout** – Vessel operators should always stay vigilant for whales and other collision hazards. Look out ahead for "blows" (puffs of mist), dorsal fins, tails, etc. Operators are further advised to post at least one dedicated whale look-out, in addition to the operator, from November through May.
- **Watch Your Speed** - NOAA recommends that vessels travel at a slow, safe speed in areas where a whale strike may occur. This speed depends on vessel type, time

Whale watching boat. *Photo credit: Belindah/Flickr.*

Whale watching from shore (O'ahu).
Photo credit: Yukihiro Matsuda/Flickr.

of day, sea conditions, and other factors that affect whale detection and avoidance. Research shows that collisions occurring at vessel speeds above 10 knots (11.5 mph or 18.5 km/hr) cause more whale deaths and serious injuries than collisions occurring at slower speeds.

- **Stay at the Helm** – Keep hands on the wheel and throttle at all times, and be ready to take action immediately to avoid a whale in your path.

- **Keep Your Distance** – Once whales are sighted, stay more than 100 yards (90 meters) away.

- **Stop Immediately** if within 100 yards (90 meters) or less of a humpback whale. Leave engines running, out of gear (in neutral) until the whale moves away.

- **Go Around Whales from Behind** while maintaining more than 100 yards distance, if you encounter whales in your path. Do not attempt to run out in front of whales to get past them.

- **Warn Other Vessels** – Use appropriate VHF radio protocol or other means to alert other vessels that may not be aware of whales in their path.

- **Don't Assume Whales See You** or will get out of the way. Calves are especially vulnerable since they are curious and may not have learned to be cautious of vessels.

- **Plan Ahead for Delays** in transit due to whale encounters; avoid nighttime operations if possible.

- **Call the NOAA Hotline if involved in a collision: 1-888-256-9840** - If a phone call is not possible, hail the US Coast Guard on VHF channel 16.

RESPONSIBLE WILDLIFE VIEWING

In addition to following the 100-yard (90-km) approach regulation and other whale protection laws, ocean-going whale-watchers should:

- Bring along binoculars and telephoto lenses to assure good views and photographs.
- While passengers may scan in all directions for whales, the vessel operator should always follow the collision avoidance guidelines.
- Once whales are sighted, slowly approach and carefully parallel alongside, while maintaining more than 100 yards (90 km) distance.
- Never operate your vessel faster than the slowest whale in the group while paralleling.
- Minimize sudden, unnecessary maneuvers or speed changes in the vicinity of whales.
- Limit your observing time to 1/2 hour or less.
- When several vessels are in the area, communicate with the other vessel operators to ensure that you do not cause disturbance.
- Please be aware that cumulative impacts may also occur. You and your vessel may not be the only one that day to have approached the same animals.
- When leaving the viewing area, slowly and vigilantly steer your vessel away – there may be other unseen whales nearby.
- Dispose of trash and vessel waste responsibly.

SIGNS OF WHALE DISTURBANCE

Cautiously move away if you observe any of the following behaviors:

- Rapid changes in swimming direction or speed.
- Erratic swimming patterns.
- Escape tactics such as prolonged diving, underwater exhalation, underwater course changes, or rapid swimming away from your location at the surface.
- Female attempting to shield calf with her body or by her movements.
- Sudden stop in important breeding, nursing, feeding or resting activities after your arrival.
- Abandonment of previously frequented areas.

ACCEPTABLE MANEUVERS

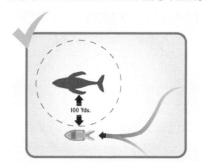

Viewing from the side: Carefully approach and parallel the whale, remaining more than 100 yards (90 km) away. If approaching from the rear, maneuver far out and to the side of the whale, before carefully viewing as above. While viewing, match the speed of the slowest whale and follow all other guidelines and regulations.

UNACCEPTABLE MANEUVERS

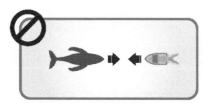

Approaching head-on: Never approach a whale head-on or in the path of the animal. If a vessel finds itself in the path of the whale, it should safely maneuver out of the path of the animal, while maintaining a distance of more than 100 yards (90 km).

Cutting a whale off from deep water.

Running in front or cutting across a whale's path.

Surrounding a whale.

Placing your vessel between a mother and calf.

Leapfrogging/Overtaking.

Signs warn boaters about the possibility of colliding with whales. *Photo credit: Cyndy Sims Parr/Flickr.*

49

FISHING

Fishing activities in federal waters are managed by the Western Pacific Regional Fisheries Management Council and NOAA Fisheries, and in state waters by the Hawai'i Department of Land and Natural Resources. The sanctuary recognizes the importance of fishing for livelihood and enjoyment in Hawai'i and currently does not have authority to regulate fishing activities within sanctuary boundaries. Additionally, the sanctuary recognizes the importance of protecting Native Hawaiian fishing and gathering rights and works to ensure they are not unnecessarily impacted by existing regulations.

Mahi mahi and ono. *Photo credit: Chris Clausen/Flickr.*

Ocean Futures Society divers Matthew Ferraro and Jacob Kilbride observe a green sea turtle.
Photo credit: Carrie Vonderhaar, Ocean Futures Society.

DIVING/SNORKELING

In addition to the humpbacks, the sanctuary is host to an impressive mix of large marine animals, such as the Hawaiian monk seal, dolphin, manta ray, green sea turtle and whitetip shark. A diverse array of topographic features, such as lava tubes, caverns and coral reefs, top off this unique diving locale, making for some of the best U.S. diving west of California. Average temperatures range from 70 to 80 °F (21 to 27 °C) with visibility between 75 and 100 feet (23-30 meters). Many commercial dive companies operate year-round from the main Hawaiian Islands.

The Fagatele Bay coastline. *Photo credit: Carrie Vonderhaar, Ocean Futures Society.*

National Marine Sanctuary of American Samoa

About the National Marine Sanctuary of American Samoa

Fagatele (pronounced fahng-ah-téh-lay) Bay's coral reefs potentially have the highest marine-life diversity of any in the sanctuary system. The Bay lies along the southern-most shore on the island of Tutuila, the largest and most populated of the seven is-lands that make up American Samoa. The Bay's beautiful fringing reefs lie in the heart of a submerged volcano, ringed by stands of dense tropical forest covering the steep cliffs that were formed when the crater was breached during the Pleistocene epoch. The depth of the crater lies at 200 feet (61 meters) beneath the surface and then plunges to 4,000 feet (1,200 meters) at the southwest drop-off. Two hundred species of corals make up the reef ecosystem that provides shelter and habitat for 1,400 spe-cies of invertebrates and algae and as many as 271 species of fish.

The National Marine Sanctuary of American Samoa[6] is comprised of six distinct units, form-ing a network of marine protected areas around the islands of the Territory of American Samoa. It is located in the cradle of Polynesia's oldest culture and is thought to support the greatest diversity of marine life in the National Marine Sanctuary System, including a wide variety of coral and other invertebrates, fishes, turtles, marine mammals and marine plants.

---

6   In 2012, National Marine Sanctuary of American Samoa completed a multi-year process to review and revise the sanctuary management plan. This effort resulted in the sanctuary expand-ing to include five additional, discreet units and a name change to the National Marine Sanctuary of American Samoa.

The sanctuary protects extensive coral reefs, including some of the oldest and largest lobe coral heads in the world, along with deep water reefs, hydrothermal vent communities, and rare marine archaeological resources, and also encompasses important fishing grounds, the southernmost point in the United States, and waters surrounding one of the world's smallest atolls. The sanctuary is also the only true tropical reef within the National Marine Sanctuary System, and is the most remote location within that system. NOAA co-manages the sanctuary with the American Samoa Government and works closely with communities adjacent to the sanctuary, all within the context of Samoan cultural traditions and practices.

Fabien and Céline Cousteau swim over delicate table corals while exploring the reefs of Fagatele Bay. *Photo credit: Carrie Vonderhaar, Ocean Futures Society.*

The sanctuary is comprised of six protected areas, covering 13,581 square miles (35,185 km2) of nearshore coral reef and offshore open ocean waters across the Samoan Archipelago. The sanctuary, among the largest of the 13 sanctuaries in the National Marine Sanctuary System was formerly the smallest, as NOAA originally established the sanctuary in 1986 to protect and preserve the 0.25 square miles of coral reef ecosystem within Fagatele Bay. In 2012, NOAA expanded the sanctuary to include Fagalua/Fogamaʻa (the next bay east of Fagatele) on Tutuila Island, as well as areas at Aunuʻu, Taʻu and Swains islands, and a marine protected area at Rose Atoll including nearby Vailuluʻu Seamount.

The Fagatele Bay portion of the sanctuary protects 163 acres (0.25 square miles or 0.65 square km) of bay area off the southwest coast of Tutuila Island, American Samoa. The landward boundary of the sanctuary is defined by the mean high water line between Fagatele Point and Steps Point. The seaward boundary is defined by a straight line between Fagatele Point and Steps Point. Maximum water depth in the sanctuary is 560 feet (170 meters), with open water depths dropping off steeply to more than 4,000 feet (1,200 meters). Due to the excellent water and habitat conditions found in the sanctuary, corals are capable of thriving at depths well beyond 100 feet (30 meters). Turtles, whales, sharks and the giant clam all find refuge in this protected area.

Fagatele Bay is a vibrant tropical reef marine ecosystem, filled with all sorts of brightly-colored tropical fish including parrot fish, damselfish and butterfly fish, as well as other sea creatures, such as lobster, crabs, sharks and octopus. From June to September, Southern humpback whales migrate north from Antarctica to calve and court in Samoan waters. Visitors can hear courting males sing whalesongs, which the whales may be using to attract mates. Several species of dolphins, as well as threatened and endangered species of sea turtles, such as the hawksbill and green sea turtle, are also frequently seen swimming in the bay. Maximum water depth in the Bay is 560 feet (170 meters), with open water depths dropping off steeply to more than 4,000 feet (1,200 meters). Due to the excellent water and habitat conditions found in the Bay, corals are capable of thriving at depths well beyond 100 feet (30 meters). Turtles, whales, sharks and the giant clam all find refuge in this protected area.

An endangered green sea turtle. *Photo credit: Carrie Vonderhaar, Ocean Futures Society.*

In June 2007, NOAA's Office of National Marine Sanctuaries completed an initial document-based maritime heritage resource inventory for American Samoa. The inventory features multiple aspects of history in American Samoa: 1) historic shipwrecks lost in American Samoa; 2) World War II naval aircraft lost in American Samoa; 3) World War II fortifications, gun emplacements, and coastal pillboxes; 4) Samoan coastal archaeological sites; and 5) coastal and marine features associated with ancient Samoan myths and legends. Very few of the historic ships or aircraft have been located within the waters of the Territory; the initial inventory work was document-based and did not involve field survey. Some of the potential sites, if located and confirmed, could be eligible for the National Register of Historic Places.

Why a National Marine Sanctuary?

Fagatele Bay is not without environmental problems, as Murphy[7] and the team learned. Outbreaks of crown-of-thorn sea stars, bleaching episodes, concerns over agricultural run-off from steep hillside plots, overfishing, and even dynamite fishing continue to threaten the reef. Yet it has withstood these onslaughts with remarkable resiliency and continues to recover where damage has occurred and even thrive where left unmolested.

Céline Cousteau, Dr. Richard Murphy and American Samoan friends inspect the reef.
Photo credit: Carrie Vonderhaar, Ocean Futures Society.

---

7   Richard Murphy, PhD, Director of Science and Education, Ocean Futures Society

Only seven-and-a-half miles (12 km) away from this little oasis lies Pago Pago, the most polluted harbor in American Samoa. Pago Pago has been ravaged by more than a century of industrialized development, but is now slowly recovering with improved sewage treatment and better management of the discharge of tuna cannery effluent. The canneries and the territorial government provide employment for the majority of Samoans who balance traditions and "progress" with as much ease as is possible for any society. Like the Bay's resilient reefs, Samoan traditions have remained largely intact despite the onslaught of outside influences. Murphy and the team met with Magele Apelu Aitaoto, High Talking Chief, who shared his perspective about the beliefs that bind Samoans together.

Descendants of Polynesian navigators, Samoan islanders have resided on the chain of seven volcanic islands since 1300 B.C. As Americans they now navigate what seems at times a disparate cultural divide. Culture and connectedness were the topics of conversation the High Talking Chief shared with Céline and Fabien. "I'd like the younger generations of Samoans to keep their culture. Go with the flow of whatever is going on with progress or whatever you call it, but at the same time, maintain the culture. We are now in a modern society, modern world where [Samoa] is no longer a remote place. We have modern technology; you can have access like anybody in New York or Australia or wherever in the world, but at the same time just keep your feet on the ground. What I mean is grab hold of your culture, keep it near to your heart, because when everything else fails, we have our land and our culture to fall back on."

Fabien and Céline Cousteau sit down for an interview with Nancy Dashbach, Ulufaleilupe Fili Fuimaomo, and Magele Apelu Aitaoto. *Photo credit: Carrie Vonderhaar, Ocean Futures Society.*

The official purpose of designating the sanctuary is "to protect and preserve an example of a pristine tropical marine habitat and coral reef terrace ecosystem of exceptional productivity, to expand public awareness and understanding of tropical marine ecosystems; to expand scientific knowledge of marine ecosystems; to improve resource management techniques, and to regulate uses within the sanctuary to ensure the health and well-being of the ecosystem and its associated flora and fauna." It was put on the list of recommended sanctuaries in 1982 and later that same year was moved to the active candidate list. The Fagatele Bay National Marine Sanctuary was designated on April 29, 1986. On October 31, 2012, NOAA designated an additional five protected areas within the sanctuary in addition to Fagatele Bay, and changed the name of the sanctuary to the National Marine Sanctuary of American Samoa

One of the underwater treasures found in the National Marine Sanctuary of American Samoa is Fagatele Bay. Access to an overview of this wonderful dive and snorkel spot is either by boat or a short walk through private property in the village of Futiga. *Photo credit: Carrie Vonderhaar, Ocean Futures Society.*

Traditional Samoan fire dance, the "Siva Afi" or "fireknife dance," which has become the symbol of Samoa. *Photo credit: Carrie Vonderhaar, Ocean Futures Society.*

Resources Within the National Marine Sanctuary of American Samoa

CORAL REEFS

Fagatele and Fagalua/Fogamaʻa bays are part of a distinct biogeographic region that is a hotspot for coral cover, coral and fish species richness, and Fagatele Bay has the highest macroalgae species diversity, and may have the highest percentage of live coral cover around Tutuila Island. Over 150 species of coral makeup the centerpiece of sanctuary marine life, which also includes over 1,400 species of other invertebrates and a wide variety of algae, several seagrasses, humpback whales and over a dozen other species of whales and dolphins, hundreds of fish species, over 30 seabird species, and hawksbill and green sea turtles. Over the past 30 years, Tutuila's reefs suffered a number of disasters that destroyed large parts of the coral reefs, including those in Fagatele Bay. In the late 1970s, an outbreak of crown-of-thorns sea star attacked the reef, destroying over 90% of the live coral. In the early 1990s, two hurricanes battered the reef that was struggling to recover from the sea star blight. Later in the 1993-94 summer, a severe bleaching event destroyed coral and other related organisms (bleaching is a response to stress—in this case hotter than normal water—where

Spinner dolphins are one species of dolphin found in American Samoa.
Photo credit: Carrie Vonderhaar, Ocean Futures Society.

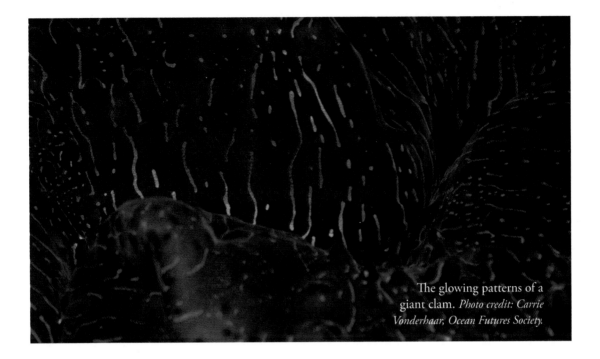

The glowing patterns of a giant clam. *Photo credit: Carrie Vonderhaar, Ocean Futures Society.*

the coral or other organism loses its microscopic symbiotic algae. If the bleached state continues for more than a few weeks, the coral will die.) Fortunately, Fagatele's reefs have shown remarkable resilience and new growth has recovered much of the devastated areas. This natural cycle of growth and destruction is typical of a tropical ecosystem.

The area surrounding Aunu'u Island has a unique fish community, and overlaps with four distinct biogeographic regions making it a highly diverse marine area that includes hot spots for coral cover, fish biomass, and fish richness. Aunu'u's Nafanua Bank is known for its coastal pelagic fish including dog-tooth tuna, giant trevally, and rainbow runner. Sanctuary waters at Aunu'u also include a vibrant patch reef system, and a coral shelf that provides a continuous habitat that extends down to deep water reefs.

The sanctuary's coral reefs at Ta'u Island include massive lobe coral heads that are among the oldest and largest known in the world, with one colony measuring 23 feet (7 m) tall and 135 feet (41 m) in circumference. The western side of Ta'u Island is a regional hotspot for coral and fish richness, possesses a distinct coral community, and shelters a large population of giant clams.

Rose Atoll is a distinct bioregion within the archipelago, is a hotspot for fish biomass, has unique coral and algal communities, supports the highest densities of giant clams in the Samoan archipelago, and is the primary site for green turtle nesting in American Samoa. The Vailuluʻu Seamount has a diverse biological community. The open ocean marine habitats around Rose Atoll are representative of the largest and the least well-protected ecosystem on earth.

Céline Cousteau examines a clownfish nestled among the coral reef. *Carrie Vonderhaar, Ocean Futures Society.*

Swains Island is a hotspot for coral cover, fish biomass and fish species richness. Its large fish biomass is high, with large schools of predators such as barracudas, jacks and snappers. Sharks and schools of humphead wrasse are frequently seen in Swains' nearshore waters, and dogtooth tuna are more common here than anywhere else in American Samoa.

Jean-Michel Cousteau and team dive the waters of Swains Island. *Photo credit: Hans Van Tilburg.*

Swains Island. *Photo credit: Wendy Cover.*

The traditional Samoan long-boat or Fautasi is 92 feet long, holds 46 men and races on special occasions.
Photo credit: Carrie Vonderhaar, Ocean Futures Society.

CULTURAL HERITAGE

Fa'a-Samoa is often heard in American Samoa. It means the Samoan Way. The culture of Samoa is over 3,000 years old. *Fa'a-Samoa* has kept Samoans strongly nationalistic and cautious about changes that might threaten the traditional structure of their way of life. However, *fa'a-Samoa* has an inherent flexibility that allows it to withstand and absorb the ways of foreign traders, missionaries, and military forces; it is a dynamic cultural force. Perhaps more than any other Polynesian culture, Samoans try to observe the traditional ways on a daily basis.

One aspect of *fa'a-Samoa* is the ancient concept of *tapu*. Samoans restricted use on areas that became overstressed in order to protect their resources. With the decline in subsistence fishing in the area, many of the new generations of Samoans have lost touch with their coral reef and its diverse riches. With the decline of awareness of *tapu*, the traditional cultural ethics of resource management were being lost as well.

The National Marine Sanctuary of American Samoa adds a new dimension to local awareness of the treasures of the marine environment and the need to protect and preserve it. By equating the sanctuary with the concept of *tapu*, a fresh understanding of resource protection and management emerges, one which can have vital cultural and environmental significance.

Key Species Within the Sanctuary

CORAL REEFS

Coral reefs are important underwater ecosystems that act as a habitat for a large number of diverse tropical fish and other sea life, including crustaceans, squid, sharks, and sea turtles. Also known as the "rainforests of the sea," coral reefs provide shelter to many of the oldest examples of life on Earth. While they cover less than 0.1 percent of the surface of the world's oceans, coral reefs sustain over one-quarter of all marine species.

New coral growth appears on the skeleton of a table coral. *Photo credit: Dr. Richard C. Murphy, Ocean Futures Society.*

Coral may look plant-like, but it is actually an animal. The Fagatele Bay coral reef contains more than 140 species of coral. Corals are cnidarians, a phylum of animals which also includes sea anemones and jellyfish. There are two groups of corals: hard corals and soft corals.

Hard corals are the true reef-building corals and are distinguished by their white limestone skeletons. It is this relatively indestructible skeleton that actually forms the coral reef, as new coral continually builds on old dead coral and the reef gradually grows.

Coral colonies grow very slowly. Under optimum conditions, massive corals may grow up to 0.8 inches (two centimeters) a year and branching corals may grow up to four inches (ten centimeters) a year. Scientists can determine the age of a coral the same way as a tree, by counting annual growth rings. Some of the corals along the Great Barrier Reef in Australia are estimated to be over 800-1000 years old.

A mushroom coral, whose retracted tentacles resemble the gills under a mushroom cap.
Photo credit: Dr. Richard C. Murphy, Ocean Futures Society.

Coral colonies can grow to be several hundred years old. *Photo credit: Carrie Vonderhaar, Ocean Futures Society.*

All corals have polyps: tiny fleshy tubes, ringed at the top by even smaller stinging tentacles. These sting the passing prey, usually plant or animal plankton, and pull it inside the tube, to the polyp's stomach. Polyps are no bigger than the size of a pencil eraser. Each polyp is an individual creature, but they live in colonies. Each polyp catches its own dinner and digests it, but the nutrients are passed along to the whole colony. Corals feed during the night, and this is the best time to see them in their full splendor. Often during the day the polyps withdraw into their hard skeletons for protection. Corals live in a symbiotic (mutually beneficial) relationship with microscopic plant cells, or algae. Coral polyps give the tiny plant cells nutrients, protection, housing, and carbon dioxide. The algae use this carbon dioxide and sunlight to make oxygen and carbohydrates, through a process called photosynthesis. The corals use the oxygen to breathe and the carbohydrates to supplement their plankton diets.

Emerging Environmental Issues

CLIMATE VARIATION AND CHANGE

Warmer oceans, ocean acidification, and changes to tropical cyclone intensity are the primary climate change drivers of concern for coral richness. Elevated ocean temperatures have the potential to negatively affect the development and survivorship of reef coral larvae. Elevated temperatures, reduced pH, and altered dissolved oxygen levels can cause serious complications for fish at multiple life stages and threaten fish richness in coral reefs. Abundant groups which may be at risk include adult and juvenile damselfish, surgeonfish, wrasse, butterfly fish, and small parrotfish.

Dr. Richard Murphy photographing the reefs in Fagatele Bay. *Photo credit: Carrie Vonderhaar, Ocean Futures Society.*

Samoan graves are built on family land, often in the front yard,
and sometimes feature spectacular views of incoming storms.
Photo credit: Carrie Vonderhaar, Ocean Futures Society.

The El Niño Southern Oscillation (ENSO) is a periodic climate phenomenon that occurs every 3-7 years. The warming phase ("El Niño") is characterized by anomalously warm seawater temperatures in the eastern Pacific Ocean and high surface pressure in the western Pacific. High rates of coral bleaching in the eastern Pacific are associated with El Niño years. The cool phase ("La Niña") exhibits an opposing pattern of surface pressure and seawater temperature. Recent work has documented the emergence of a new El Niño signature that exhibits significant trends with ongoing anthropogenic climate change. The central Pacific El Niño (CP-El Niño) refers to conditions of warm sea surface temperatures in the central Pacific flanked by cooler sea surface temperatures to the west and east. Under global warming, the occurrence of CP-El Niño is projected to increase as much as five times. The effect of increased incidence of CP-El Niño is not fully understood but would result in greater sea surface temperatures in the central Pacific region accompanied by a westerly shift in rainfall trends. Increased temperature and other stressors are known to cause coral bleaching—a phenomenon where the symbiotic algae found within many corals are lost. Bleached corals appear white in color. Prolonged periods of bleaching without recovery eventually lead to the death of the coral.

This image depicts corals in various stages of health. The coral on the left side of the photo is green, indicating healthy coral that contains symbiotic zooxanthellae algae. On the right, the coral is in the process of dying, as indicated by the bleached central portion of the coral, surrounded by a band of green. The purple colored corals in the photo are also undergoing the bleaching process. The coral in the center dramatically shows a completely bleached coral, indicated by the white color and complete absence of zooxanthellae. *Photo credit: Dr. Richard C. Murphy, Ocean Futures Society.*

Since the 1970s, global cyclone destructiveness has increased in the western north Pacific and north Atlantic, resulting in increased peak wind velocities and precipitation. Because small increases in wind speed disproportionately increase the destructive power of a cyclone (destructive power increases with wind speed), more recent cyclones have exhibited approximately double the destructive force of earlier cyclones. Even infrequent cyclonic storms can have a major impact on coral reef communities. With increasing sea surface temperatures, there is greater energy available to feed these cyclonic storms, increasing their detrimental impact. These storms also bring increased sedimentation and nutrients into the reefs, which can smother and kill coral as well as fuel algal blooms.

Increased atmospheric carbon dioxide levels have resulted in ocean acidification, a term that describes the general decrease in pH and alteration to the chemical balance of the ocean. Ocean acidification affects a variety of processes in marine organisms. Most studied has been the effect of acidification on calcification in corals and invertebrates. This is of great importance because calcifying organisms are ubiquitous, with calcifying representatives found in the crustaceans, mollusks, echinoderms and corals, among many others. Ocean acidification may also influence other physiological processes such as sensory capabilities as well as the ability to cope with other stressors such as temperature increases.

Algae can overgrow and smother corals on tropical reefs.
Photo credit: NOAA.

Impacts of climate variability and change on Fagatele Bay's coral reef systems could include the following:

- A shift of coral distribution away from shallow water into deeper (cooler) areas
- Successful establishment of new non-native marine species, which could potentially compete with native species
- Increasing outbreaks of diseases
- Increased rates of coral bleaching
- Changes in the timing of reproductive (spawning) events
- Decreased ability of corals, crabs, calcareous algae and other calcifying organisms to build skeletons
- Increased siltation

Céline Cousteau points out a calcifying organism on the coral reef: the giant clam.
Photo credit: Carrie Vonderhaar, Ocean Futures Society.

Fabien and Céline Cousteau dive the coral reef in Fagatele Bay.
Photo credit: Carrie Vonderhaar, Ocean Futures Society.

Tuna Cannery. *Photo credit:*
Carrie Vonderhaar, Ocean Futures Society.

Marine debris accumulates on the
underwater coastline, such as this suitcase
found by Fabien Cousteau. *Photo credit:*
Carrie Vonderhaar, Ocean Futures Society.

WATER QUALITY

"My impression of Fagatele Bay's reefs was that they are resilient and much healthier than many we've seen in Hawai'i and the Caribbean, where only small corals and algae dominate the bottom. Having lost much of the resiliency, they struggle to recover from destructive events, while Fagatele Bay's reefs rapidly bounce back.

"In contrast to this were the reefs around the harbor of Pago Pago. Here the water was turbid, sediments covered corals, and most corals were small. In the past, tuna canneries dumped their waste directly into the harbor and pretty much destroyed the healthy reefs there. Now the cannery waste is dumped offshore and normal biota appears to be returning.

"At least both the water conditions and the reefs have improved. Although surveys of the harbor reefs were conducted as long ago as 1928, the harbor has been a major port since the late 1800s, so it's difficult to know what "normal" really is here. In spite of the present conditions though, we saw that hardy corals, which are tolerant to nutrients and sediments, are thriving. The most depressing aspect of these reefs was the amount of debris. We found used tires, cans, diapers, shopping carts, plastic, and even a suitcase. This is totally avoidable and requires public education to help people understand the consequences of being careless." [Richard Murphy, Ocean Futures Society]

Crown-of-thorns sea star. *Photo credit: Carrie Vonderhaar, Ocean Futures Society.*

CROWN-OF-THORNS SEA STAR

The crown-of-thorns sea star ("alamea" in the Samoan language), preys on coral. Usually, these starfish are a rare member of the reef community; however, plagues of crown-of-thorns sea star can occur rapidly and kill large tracts of coral. In 1978 and 1979, an outbreak of crown-of-thorns sea star devastated coral populations on Tutuila's reefs. The massive infestation resulted in a loss of more than 90 percent of all the living corals in Fagatele Bay. At the time, Fagatele Bay was not a sanctuary, but this disaster helped to propel the decision for the site's designation.

The soft tissues of coral are consumed when crown-of-thorns sea star feeds, leaving behind the hard coral skeleton. As long as other aspects of the ecosystem are intact and new disturbances do not occur, new coral recruitment and growth may replace the damage caused by the sea star. The reefs of Fagatele Bay are resilient because coralline algae rapidly colonizes the dead coral skeletons and cements reef surfaces together to promote the settlement and growth of new coral colonies. Without this rapid colonization by coralline algae, wave action can cause the dead coral skeletons to fragment and turn to rubble before the new coral community can establish. Continued pressure from human impacts coupled with the addition of climate change stressors may decrease the resilience of coral reefs in Fagatele Bay to recover from crown-of-thorns outbreaks.

Research Within the Sanctuary

Research in the National Marine Sanctuary of American Samoa focuses on two main topics: factors affecting the health of the coral reef ecosystem and studies of large marine mammals in the area.

- **Coral reef long-term survey**: Spurred by the crown-of-thorns invasion in the 1970's, scientists have been conducting long-term research in Fagatele Bay to monitor the recovery of coral reefs. Because corals grow slowly, the research team chose a multi-year cycle of data collection. Beginning in 1985, and again in 1988, 1995, 1998, 2001, 2004, and 2007, the team amassed information on coral, fishes, invertebrates and marine plants. This database is unique for Samoa and the study is one of the few long-running surveys of its type in the world.

- **Humpback whale research:** Since 2003, an annual survey of Tutuila's marine mammals focusing on the humpback whales that visit each winter has been conducted by the Hawaiian Islands Humpback Whale National Marine Sanctuary's Research Coordinator. In cooperation with other local agencies, researchers have gathered photos and skin samples of dozens of humpback whales, expanding our knowledge about this species. The photos help to identify individual animals: humpback flukes, or tails, are distinctive for every individual like human fingerprints. Skin samples provide additional information including the sex, the reproductive status of a female, and what types of fat-soluble pollutants are in their bodies. Scientists are discovering that humpbacks are more abundant in Samoa than formerly believed. These 45-foot (14-meter) mammals travel to American Samoa waters each winter from June through October. They come here to calve and nurse their young in the sheltered bays of the islands until the calves are large enough to undertake the long trek back to the Antarctic feeding grounds. Males vie for the attention of females, and although mating has never been observed, the females are pregnant by the time they reach Antarctica.

Two divers are towed behind a small boat
in order to survey a large area of coral reef.
Photo credit: Dr. Jean Kenyon, NOAA Fisheries.

Humpback whales often calve and breed in Samoan waters. *Photo credit: Paul Brown.*

Research Assets

R/V *MANUMĀ*

The sanctuary currently operates one vessel in support of research and monitoring, education and emergency response. The R/V *Manumā* is a multi-purpose research vessel designed primarily to support sanctuary science and education missions. It also supports researchers from the National Park Service, American Samoa Department of Marine and Wildlife Resources, and other sanctuary partners.

This rigid-hull inflatable has an overall length of 33 feet (10 meters). It carries a crew of two to three and a science party of five to seven for single day trips. Since it was acquired in 2009, the vessel has served as a platform for research and monitoring from diving operations to benthic habitat mapping, and for regional damage assessments and recovery efforts following the September 2009 tsunami. It is the only NOAA platform dedicated to marine research in the territory.

The R/V Manumā. *Photo credit: NOAA.*

Visiting the Sanctuary

Note: In the last section of the book, "When You Visit the Sanctuaries," is detailed information about resources found within each sanctuary to help visitors have an enjoyable and productive visit.

VISITOR'S CENTER

Tauese P.F. Sunia Ocean Center   Open Monday to Friday 9 a.m. – 4 p.m.
Utulei, American Samoa.   Open Saturdays 9 a.m. – 12 p.m.
Telephone: (684) 633-6500   **Admission is free.**

The National Marine Sanctuary held a grand opening ceremony for the Tauese P.F. Sunia Ocean Center on August 17, 2012. The Ocean Center provides visitors and residents with opportunity to learn about the natural and cultural resources of American Samoa. The state-of-the-art facility features educational exhibits and interactive learning tools to promote ocean awareness and encourage good marine stewardship.

The National Marine Sanctuary, in collaboration with the American Samoa Department of Commerce, has installed two educational kiosks highlighting the importance of marine resource protection in American Samoa. The kiosks are located in the waiting lounge at Pago Pago International Airport, and Lyndon B. Johnson Tropical Medical Center. Underscoring the sanctuary's commitment to outreach and education, the kiosks provide a visual and interactive showcase of the sanctuary's underwater treasures. With the click of a button, users can obtain extensive information about marine species and habitats, and learn about various sanctuary activities, educational and outreach programs, research projects and resource protection programs. The kiosks also include a "Kids Corner" where children can see and learn about marine life in a fun and entertaining way.

Regional office location
National Marine Sanctuary of American Samoa
P.O. Box 4318
Pago Pago, American Samoa 96799
Telephone: 684-633-6500

Visiting the National Marine Sanctuary of American Samoa is difficult even in good weather because of its remote location. One can approach Fagatele Bay either by boat from Pago Pago or Leone Bay, or by car and then follow the trail down the western wall. Fagatele Bay can be accessed from the village of Futiga Monday to Friday, 7.30 a.m to 4.00 p.m and Saturday, 7.30 a.m to 1.30 p.m. The Bay is closed on Sundays unless arrangements have been made at least 48 hours in advance through the sanctuary staff.

The land surrounding the Bay belongs to the Fuimaono family which has lived near the Bay's slopes for thousands of years. Public access to the Bay is from the main highway within the village of Futiga. Visitors will turn off onto a dirt road that passes the landfill (2 miles/3km inland), and veer past a vegetable farm area to a gate. The only homestead,

Tauese P.F. Sunia Ocean Center. *Photo credit: NOAA/National Marine Sanctuaries.*

Educational kiosks. *Photo credit: Emily Gaskin, NOAA/ National Marine Sanctuaries.*

on the right, is occupied by the assigned caretaker of family lands – Mr. Pio Fuimaono. All vehicles must be parked within the allotted parking area on Pio Fuimaono's land. No parking overnight, or after operational hours, is allowed.

Protocol for Land Access to the Bay

Interested visitors or groups to the Bay must check in with Mr. Fuimaono prior to passing beyond the gate, register in the log book and receive an informational brochure about the National Marine Sanctuary of American Samoa. Vehicle access beyond the gate is not allowed unless under special conditions/exemptions. The distance from the gate to the first educational sign is 1.2 miles (2 km). It is an additional 0.9 miles (1.5 km) from this spot to the bay. Other trails from the bay to Fagalua or to Taputimu are accessible by foot, with a total distance approximately 3 miles (5 km) long. There is no charge for access to Fagatele Bay.

Dress Code

Visitors should plan to dress lightly. Casual summer clothing—sandals, shorts and short sleeved shirts are suggested. Rain gear is always appropriate, but because of the region's high humidity visitors may get just as wet wearing a raincoat as not. People who are planning to hike should wear sturdy boots. Since the islands are volcanic in nature, lava rubble is found every-

Signs line the trail leading to Fagatele Bay. Photo credit: Veronika Mortenson, NOAA/National Marine Sanctuaries.

where; it can be rough on lesser quality boots and shoes. Visitors should bring their own snorkel equipment.

NOTE: It is customary in Samoa to cover much of the body. It is expected that men and women cover their shoulders and knees. Even when swimming, visitors are asked to wear modest clothing; no bikinis, please.

ECO-TOURS

Visitors who are interested in participating in guided tours of the National Marine Sanctuary of American Samoa should check with the sanctuary office. Some hotels may also offer tours to guests.

BOATING

Two mooring buoys were installed in Fagatele Bay in 2006 to allow boaters to visit the bay without dropping anchor. Anchoring is prohibited within the sanctuary.

Two divers place a mooring buoy in the sanctuary. Mooring buoys allow boats to tie onto them, in order to prevent anchor damage to living oral. *Photo credit: Mike Smith.*

FISHING

Fishing is not allowed in Fagatele Bay. Other regions of the sanctuary have specific fishing restrictions. Giant clams and live rock are protected in most locations. Visitors wishing to fish in the sanctuary should contact the sanctuary office for rules in the area they plan to visit.

DIVING/SNORKELING

Local residents and tourists visit Fagatele Bay to snorkel and, less frequently, to dive. The water visibility in the bay is normally around 70 feet (21 meters).

Dusky anemonefish, a type of clownfish.
Photo credit: Carrie Vonderhaar, Ocean Futures Society.

Papahānaumokuākea Marine National Monument

About Papahānaumokuākea Marine National Monument

Papahānaumokuākea Marine National Monument is the single largest conservation area under the U.S. flag, and one of the largest marine conservation areas in the world. First encompassing 139,797 square miles (362,073 km^2) of the Pacific Ocean around the Northwestern Hawaiian Islands (NWHI), it now stretches over 582,578 square miles (1,508,870 km^2)—an area four times larger than all the country's national parks combined.

A double rainbow appears at East Island while Sooty Terns fly by. *Photo credit: Tom Ordway, Ocean Futures Society.*

Beyond the main eight populated islands of Hawai'i lies a string of tiny islands, atolls, shoals, and banks spanning 1,200 miles (1,930 km) of the Pacific Ocean, the world's largest body of water. Hundreds of miles northwest of Kaua'i, places like Nihoa, Laysan, Pearl and Hermes, and Kure comprise the little known, rarely visited Northwestern Hawaiian Islands. Seen from space, the area's shallow waters appear as a string of turquoise jewels in an empty and dark blue vastness. If they were laid atop the continental United States, the NWHI would cover a distance equal to that between New York City and Omaha, or Boston and the Florida Everglades.

Thanks to their isolation, these 4,500 square miles (11,650 km²) of wild coral reefs are among the healthiest and most extensive in the world. This marine wilderness is home to the highly endangered Hawaiian monk seal, the world's second most endangered seal, and uninhabited sandy islets provide the nesting grounds for more than 90 percent of Hawai'i's threatened green sea turtles. Though land areas are limited, over 14 million seabirds nest here.

Terns, terns, terns, and a few other kinds of birds on Tern Island. Hawai'i, Papahānaumokuākea Marine National Monument. *Photo credit: Nancy Marr, Ocean Futures Society.*

A male masked angelfish is valued at $7,000.00 in the aquarium trade. Fortunately, they are protected in the Papahānaumokuākea Marine National Monument. *Photo credit: Tom Ordway, Ocean Futures Society.*

The marine habitats of the NWHI contain features not found in the main Hawaiian Islands, such as coral atolls, and nurture thriving populations of many species once abundant in the main Hawaiian Islands, but rarely found today. Large predatory fish such as jacks, Hawaiian grouper, and sharks are nearly fifteen times as numerous in the shallow waters of NWHI compared to the heavily fished main Hawaiian Islands. Many sought-after aquarium species, now rare in the main Hawaiian Islands, are much more common on these reefs as well.

Laysan duck on Midway Atoll National Wildlife Refuge in Papahānaumokuākea Marine National Monument. *Photo credit: Andy Collins, NOAA.*

The extensive coral reefs found in Papahānaumokuākea—truly the rainforests of the sea—are home to over 7,000 marine species, one quarter of which are found only in the Hawaiian Archipelago. Many of the islands and shallow water environments are important habitats for rare species such as the threatened green turtle and the endangered Hawaiian monk seal. On less than six square miles (15 km²) of land, over 14 million seabirds representing 22 species breed and nest. Land areas also provide a home for four species of bird found nowhere else in the world, including the world's most endangered duck, the Laysan duck.

Papahānaumokuākea is of great cultural importance to Native Hawaiians with significant cultural sites found on the islands of Nihoa and Mokumanamana, both of which are on the National and State Register for Historic Places. Mokumanamana has the highest density of sacred sites in the Hawaiian Archipelago and has spiritual significance in Hawaiian cosmology. During their trans-Pacific voyages, ancient Polynesians sailed these waters and used these islands for centuries as places of residence and worship. When Western explorers found these islands they raced to claim them for their own nations. Entrepreneurs tried to make a living from natural resources found there, and the world's first global communications network linked through these islands.

The whaling industry transformed the Hawaiian Islands in the early 19th century. Vessels stopped in Honolulu ports for provisions and to recruit new whalers. At one time, Native Hawaiians comprised nearly one-fifth of the sailors in the Pacific-based American whaling fleet.

Nihoa Island. *Photo credit: Tom Ordway, Ocean Futures Society.*

A trypot discovered by NOAA archaeologists at the Nantucket whaleship Two Brothers, wrecked in 1823. Trypots were used aboard whaling ships to render whale blubber into oil. *Photo credit: Tane Casserley/NOAA.*

Sailors began to travel thousands of miles and for years at a time in search of new whaling grounds across the globe as whales became scarce from decades of overfishing. When the Japan whaling grounds were discovered around 1820, ships began sailing through the low-lying atolls of the Northwestern Hawaiian Islands in search of "liquid gold" (whale oil) just beyond Kure Atoll. At least ten whaling vessels were reported lost in the Northwestern Hawaiian Islands, including the *Parker*, *Gledstanes*, the *Two Brothers*, and the *Pearl* and the *Hermes*. To date, five of these whaling ships have been located and investigated by NOAA maritime archaeologists.

At least 67 naval aircraft are recorded as being lost in the vicinity of the NWHI. World War II played a large role in these losses. The Navy built a Naval Air Facility at Midway Atoll beginning in 1940; Eastern Island had the main airfield in the early days of the war and the submarine and seaplane support operations were concentrated on Sand Island. This was a vital center for submarine, surface and aviation operations. Initially, the Hawaiian Sea Frontier forces stationed patrol vessels at most of the islands and atolls. Midway was also the focus of one of the most important naval battles in the Pacific. The Battle of Midway took place from June 4-7, 1942 and is considered the turning point of the war in the Pacific. The majority of the sea battle took place beyond the NWHI between 100 to 200 miles to the north, but an intense air fight was waged directly over and around the atoll itself. Numerous Japanese and American planes splashed down into Midway waters. Many of these sites are war graves. Training exercises before and after the battle also took their toll.

A diver inspecting the remains of the USS MACAW at Midway Atoll. Hawai'i, Papahānaumokuākea Marine National Monument. *Photo credit: Robert Schwemmer, NOAA.*

For Native Hawaiians, place names are an important way to preserve information about an area's geology, its history, natural and supernatural phenomenon specific to it, or its uses by gods and men. The name Papahānaumokuākea was given to the region by a group of Native Hawaiian cultural practitioners and kūpuna (elders) one year after the area was designated as a Marine National Monument. The name specifically relates to one of the stories contained within the Kumulipo[8], which

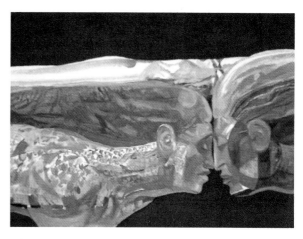

The birth of the Hawaiian Islands and Native Hawaiian people. *Artwork by: Solomon Enos.*

tells the story of Papahānaumoku (a mother figure who is personified in the earth) and Wākea (a father figure who is personified in the expansive sky). These two figures, either together or separately, are responsible for the creation or birthing of the entire archipelago, and they are the most recognized ancestors of the Native Hawaiian people. The name Papahānaumokuākea is reflective of the region's natural and cultural heritage and its future as a vast, sacred, protected and procreative place. The preservation of these names, together, as Papahānaumokuākea, strengthens Hawai'i's cultural foundation and grounds Hawaiians to an important part of their historical past. Taken apart, "Papa" (earth mother), "hānau" (birth), "moku" (small island or land division), and "ākea" (wide) bespeak a fertile woman giving birth to a wide stretch of islands beneath a benevolent sky, the dramatic imagery of which is on full display in the region.

The Monument vision is to forever protect and perpetuate ecosystem health and diversity and Native Hawaiian cultural significance of Papahānaumokuākea. The Monument mission is to carry out seamless integrated management to ensure ecological integrity and achieve strong, long-term protection and perpetuation of Northwestern Hawaiian Islands ecosystems, Native Hawaiian culture, and heritage resources for current and future generations.

---

8   a chant in the Hawaiian language telling a creation story

Why a Marine National Monument?

For millions of years the Northwestern Hawaiian Islands (NWHI) remained in a pristine natural state, drifting northwestward atop the Pacific Plate at about 3.2 inches (8.1 cm) per year, and slowly eroding back into the sea. Over time, new species arrived, mostly from the south; some adapted to the new surroundings while others went extinct. Early Polynesian voyagers, in their epic trans-Pacific voyages aboard large double-hulled sailing canoes, were the first humans to arrive in these Northwestern islands as early as 1000 A.D. Evidence of permanent living sites exists only for Nihoa, with temporary settlement and cultural sites found on Mokumanamana. Early Hawaiians lived on Nihoa for an estimated 700 years, but this occupation mysteriously ceased before Captain Cook's first landing in Hawai'i in 1778.

These islands provide breeding sites for all but three of Hawai'i's 23 species of seabirds, such as the gray-backed tern, short-tailed albatross, and the red-tailed tropicbird. Millions of central Pacific seabirds congregate on these islands to breed. They nest in burrows and cliffs, on the ground, and in trees and shrubs. For some species, these tiny specks of land provide their only breeding site.

Jean-Michel Cousteau visits the ceremonial site, or wahi pana, on the island of Mokumanamana.
Photo credit: Nan Marr, Ocean Futures Society.

Laysan Albatross eggs collected for harvest in the early 1890's. *Photo Credit: Hawai'i State Archives.*

The eighteenth and nineteenth centuries brought increased international trade and commerce within Hawaiian waters, which in turn increased the exploitation of both the animal species and the terrestrial environments of the NWHI. Seabirds were harvested for their feathers by the hundreds of thousands. Albatross eggs were also collected, and the sand and coral rubble islands were mined for guano, which was processed into fertilizer. Entire island ecosystems were completely destroyed by over harvesting and the introduction of new species, such as rabbits to Laysan Island.

Many species of plants and animals still exist in Papahānaumokuākea that once occurred in the main Hawaiian Islands (as evidenced by their presence in the fossil record), but could not survive after the arrival of humans and their associated mammals. In all, there are 23 species found in Papahānaumokuākea Marine National Monument that are listed under the U.S. Endangered Species Act, and there are undoubtedly many more that might be eligible for listing.

Papahānaumokuākea is characterized by a high degree of endemism in reef fish species, particularly at the northern end of the chain, and corals. Over 50% of the reef fish (by numerical abundance) found in the three northernmost atolls are endemic to the Hawaiian Archipelago; 30% of all corals found in the NWHI are found only in Hawai'i. No other coral reefs of similar size and expanse on the planet have a higher rate of endemism than Hawai'i's. Given the balancing act that coral reefs must maintain, and their fragile structure, they are very susceptible to disturbances, such as overfishing, shoreline development, storms, and pollution. Coral reefs around the world are in serious decline and many are heavily compromised.

An endangered short-tailed albatross on Sand Island, Midway Atoll National Wildlife Refuge. A pair of short-tailed albatross on Eastern Island gave birth to the first short-tailed albatross recorded outside of Japan in 2011. *Photo credit: Andy Collins NOAA Office of National Marine Sanctuaries.*

Jean-Michel Cousteau leads the way through the tight grottos at the north end of Pearl and Hermes.
Photo credit: Tom Ordway, Ocean Futures Society.

Most reef systems around the world have seen a dramatic reduction of large predatory fish, and this is disturbing, since healthy populations of predator species are a good indicator of an ecosystem's overall health. When predator populations are greatly reduced by fishing and other human activities, the normal structure of the reef community is disrupted. More than half the weight (biomass) of all fish on Papahānaumokuākea coral reefs consists of large top-level predators like sharks and jacks. In contrast, only three percent of the fish biomass on the main Hawaiian Islands' reefs is composed of these predatory fish, several of which are highly prized food and game fishes. It is likely that this difference results from human impacts such as fishing and habitat loss from shoreline development. These activities, largely absent in Papahānaumokuākea, make it one of the last places on Earth where scientists can study the ecology of a coral reef ecosystem without large-scale human disturbance. Such studies provide new insights into how Hawaiian coral reef ecosystems function, and the impacts of removing large predators.

Galapagos shark (Mano.) *Photo credit: Tom Ordway, Ocean Futures Society.*

Hawaiian monk seals are found only in Hawai'i , with the main breeding subpopulations located throughout the Northwestern Hawaiian Islands and a small but growing population in the main Hawaiian Islands. This population represents one of only two monk seal populations remaining anywhere, as the monk seals of the Caribbean are extinct and the populations of the Mediterranean monk seals are very low—estimated at approximately 600 individuals. In 1988, the National Marine Fisheries Service designated critical habitat for the Hawaiian monk seal from shore to 20 fathoms (120 feet or 37 meters) around every island, atoll, and bank of Papahānaumokuākea, except Sand Island at Midway Atoll. This habitat includes "all beach areas, sand spits and islets, inner reef waters, and ocean waters."

Endangered Hawaiian monk seal.
Photo credit: Tom Ordway, Ocean Futures Society.

East Island at French Frigate Shoals is the most important nesting area for green turtles in Hawai'i. More than 800 nesters were counted in 2011. *Photo credit: Andy Collins, NOAA Office of National Marine Sanctuaries.*

Papahānaumokuākea also provides nearly the entire nesting habitat for the threatened Hawaiian green sea turtle. On the undisturbed beaches of these remote atolls, both male and female turtles come ashore to bask on the beach in broad daylight, a behavior no longer seen in most other parts of the world. The critically endangered hawksbill and leatherback turtles, and the endangered olive ridley and loggerhead turtles, are also found in Papahānaumokuākea. In addition, the waters of Papahānaumokuākea are home to more than 20 whale and dolphin species, six of them federally and/or internationally recognized as endangered. Recent research indicates that Papahānaumokuākea contains two-thirds of the potential humpback whale wintering habitat in the Hawaiian Archipelago. This study documented for the first time breeding and calving activity of humpback whales within Papahānaumokuākea.

Welcome sign to Midway Atoll.
Photo credit: Susie Holst, NOAA Coral Reef Conservation Program.

President Theodore Roosevelt created the Hawaiian Islands Reservation in 1909 as a response to overharvesting of seabirds, and in recognition of the islands' importance as seabird nesting grounds. Subsequently, the reservation became the Hawaiian Islands National Wildlife Refuge. President Roosevelt's action was the first in a series of incremental protections for the NWHI, and adjacent marine habitats, leading up to the establishment of Midway Atoll National Wildlife Refuge in 1988, Kure Atoll State Wildlife Sanctuary in 1993 and the NWHI Coral Reef Ecosystem Reserve in 2000.

The Executive Orders that created the Reserve in 2000 also initiated a process to designate the waters of the NWHI as a federal national marine sanctuary. Public meetings to discuss the proposed sanctuary were held in 2002. Support for the protection and preservation of the Northwestern Hawaiian Islands was overwhelming, with more than 52,000 public comments submitted during the five years of the proposed national marine sanctuary designation process, the majority in favor of strong protection.

In 2005, Governor Linda Lingle signed regulations establishing a state marine refuge in the near-shore waters of the NWHI (out to three miles/five kilometers, except Midway Atoll) that excluded all extractive uses of the region, except those permitted for research or other purposes that benefited management.

On June 15, 2006, President George W. Bush issued Presidential Proclamation 8031, creating the Northwestern Hawaiian Islands Marine National Monument, having been inspired to do so, in part, by a recent screening of the "Voyage to Kure" section of the documentary series *Jean-Michel Cousteau: Ocean Adventures*. The President's actions followed Governor Lingle's lead and immediately afforded the NWHI the nation's highest form of marine environmental protection. Protection was effective immediately and includes requiring permits for access into the monument. Protections also include the prohibition of commercial and recreational harvest of precious coral, crustaceans and coral reef species in monument waters; the prohibition of oil, gas and mineral exploration and extraction anywhere in the monument; the prohibition of waste dumping; and the phase-out of commercial fishing in monument waters over a five-year period. In February 2007, the President amended the Proclamation, renaming the monument Papahānaumokuākea Marine National Monument, to reflect native Hawaiian language and culture. All commercial fishing ceased in 2010, and the fisheries remain closed as per terms of the Presidential Proclamation.

In 2016, President Obama used his final months in office to quadruple the size of the Papahānaumokuākea Marine National Monument—from 140,000 square miles in size to over 580,000 square miles—further safeguarding the thousands of marine and terrestrial species found there.

President George W. Bush signed a proclamation to create the Northwestern Hawaiian Islands Marine National Monument at a ceremony Wednesday, June 15, 2006, in the East Room of the White House. *Photo credit: National Marine Sanctuary Foundation.*

Managed jointly by the U.S. Fish and Wildlife Service, the National Oceanic and Atmospheric Administration (NOAA), and the state of Hawai'i, Papahānaumokuākea is the largest single area dedicated to conservation in the history of our country and the largest protected marine area in the world. It is...larger than all of our National Parks combined. The designation was unprecedented in the scale of strict rules attached to it, including the phasing out of commercial fishing (sport fishing was already prohibited) in five years.

Delegates to the United Nations Educational, Scientific and Cultural Organization's (UNESCO) 34th World Heritage Convention in Brasilia, Brazil, agreed July 30, 2010 to inscribe Papahānaumokuākea Marine National Monument as one of only 28 mixed (natural and cultural) World Heritage Sites in the World. Globally, Papahānaumokuākea is also one of only 47 marine sites. Inscription of this remote oceanic expanse was the first nomination of a United States site in 15 years. The vote also established the first mixed World Heritage Site in the nation.

Resources Within the Papahānaumokuākea Marine National Monument

CORAL REEFS

Often called the "rainforests" of the sea, coral reefs are vital to maintaining the biological diversity of our oceans. They are highly complex and productive ecosystems composed of countless millions of plants and animals dependent upon one another to survive. Building layer upon layer, coral reefs form an intricate living tapestry with more species per unit area than any other marine environment. Though coral reefs compose only about 0.2 percent of the ocean's floor, scientists have estimated that they shelter and support nearly one million species of fish, invertebrates, and algae; many yet to be discovered.

The living coral reef colonies of the Papahānaumokuākea Marine National Monument are a spectacular underwater landscape covering thousands of square miles. These reefs are some of the healthiest and least disturbed coral reefs remaining and comprise the last large-scale, predator-dominated coral reef ecosystems on the planet. Over millennia, invertebrate animals and algae have constructed massive structures in the shallow seas. Coral animals, bonded to basalt from ancient volcanoes, secreted skeletons of calcium carbonate that formed the substance of which reefs are built. The basaltic islands eventually eroded away and subsided under their massive weight. However, the upward growth of the coral reefs kept pace with the gradual sinking of the volcanic remnants, creating shallow reefs that rise to the surface of the ocean but no further. The reefs and atolls we see today represent the "footprints" of former high volcanic islands.

The Papahānaumokuākea coral reefs are the foundation of an ecosystem that hosts more than 7,000 species, including marine mammals, fishes, sea turtles, birds, and invertebrates. Many are rare, threatened, or endangered. At least one quarter are endemic, found nowhere else on the planet. Many more remain unidentified or even unknown to science. Unexplored deep-sea habitats, expensive and challenging to survey, may provide new species records to science for decades. Even the shallow coral reef habitats hold species new to science. This is especially true for invertebrates and algae.

A perfect image that reflects all the key components of a healthy coral reef ecosystem.
Photo credit: Tom Ordway, Ocean Futures Society.

Schools of colorful damselfish are abundant near this reef structure.
Photo credit: Tom Ordway, Ocean Futures Society.

Coral reefs provide resources and services worth billions of dollars to economies world-wide. In many coastal communities adjacent to coral reefs, people rely on the reef's bounty for the majority of their food. Around the main Hawaiian Islands, coral reefs protect the shores from storms, and they shape the waves that inspired the sport of surfing, now exported worldwide. U.S. residents say Hawai'i's coral reef ecosystems are worth $33.57 billion per year.

For all their biological richness and economic value, coral reefs are fragile environments that remain healthy only within a narrow window of ocean and climatic conditions. Seawater a few degrees hotter or colder than what corals are accustomed to can impact their survival, and they need clean, clear water in order to get the sunlight they need to produce food. Corals are also sensitive to physical disturbance, since only the thin outer layer of the coral structure is living tissue. Within coral reefs, plants and animals compete for limited space and food, and a delicate balance has developed over time among species. This fragile balance can be easily disturbed if one or more species are removed or depleted, allowing another species to grow unchecked. In some cases, such as when algae eaters like manini (convict tang), cowries, or sea urchins are removed, the limu (algae) can grow so rapidly that it overgrows and smothers the corals. These "lawnmowers of the reef" help keep reefs in balance, and are but one thread in an intricate web of life.

Honey cowry shell. The Hawaiian name is leho opule. Photo credit: Dr. Dwayne Meadows, NOAA Fisheries, Office of Protected Resouces.

Jean-Michel Cousteau makes friends with one of the many Laysan albatross on Midway Atoll in the Papahānaumokuākea Marine National Monument. *Photo credit: Tom Ordway, Ocean Futures Society.*

ISLANDS

The terrestrial area of Papahānaumokuākea is very small compared to its marine area, and only the larger and higher islands are of sufficient size to support significant and diverse plant life. All islands are dry, with minimal fresh water resources. Remarkably, given these limitations, the terrestrial areas of Papahānaumokuākea support significant endemism. All the islands and atolls of Papahānaumokuākea except Gardner Pinnacles, Maro Reef and Midway support endemic species that are specific to their respective islands. This includes at least 145 species of arthropods, six species of endangered plants, and four types of birds, including remarkably isolated species such as the Nihoa finch, Nihoa millerbird, Laysan finch, and the Laysan duck, one of the world's rarest ducks. Three of these species (Nihoa finch, Nihoa millerbird, and Laysan duck) are deemed critically endangered by the International Union for Conservation of Nature (IUCN), and the Laysan finch is listed as vulnerable. More than 14 million seabirds nest, rest and breed on the tiny islets in the chain, including 99% of the world's Laysan albatrosses (listed as vulnerable by the IUCN) and 98% of the world's black-footed albatrosses (listed as endangered by the IUCN).

A close up of the endemic Laysan finch. *Photo credit: Tom Ordway, Ocean Futures Society.*

Endangered Nihoa fan palm on the island of Nihoa. *Photo credit: David Boynton.*

The plants of the NWHI are primarily coastal strand species of the Pacific that can tolerate high salt levels, periodic drought, and intense sun. Most have seeds capable of dispersing in seawater. Some plants evolved into new species, and six endemic plants are listed under the Endangered Species Act, including the endangered Nihoa fan palm. A similar palm went extinct during the rabbit plague on Laysan Island, and in recent years an alien grasshopper has attacked Nihoa's palms.

The first entomologists (insect scientists) visited Laysan Island in 1893, and upon numerous subsequent visits, identified at least 75 native species, including 15 found only on Laysan. The arthropods and land snails are the least understood components of the terrestrial ecosystems, but studies continue to improve our knowledge. At least 35 species of endemic insects and spiders, and six species of endemic land snails have been identified at Nihoa Island. Unfortunately, positive discoveries are at times offset by negative ones – as many as 125 species of alien insects and spiders have also been found, and some of these, particularly ants, are extremely destructive. Considered "ecosystem busters," introduced ants have the ability to displace native species, and even affect the survival of ground nesting seabirds.

CULTURAL HERITAGE

The Papahānaumokuākea Marine National Monument contains historic shipwreck sites, heritage resources which capture the region's seafaring past in graphic detail. More than 100 vessels and aircraft are known to have been lost in this region. Systematic survey of these sites began in 2002. Each wreck site is like a time capsule, allowing a glimpse of a part of seafaring history.

Dr. Kelly Gleason with ginger jar from Two Brothers shipwreck.
Photo credit: Greg McFall, NOAA National Marine Sanctuaries.

The wrecks of American and British whaling ships lost during the early decades of the 19th century depict the many hazards associated with seafaring. The debris trail of the American whaler *Parker*, lost in 1842 during a violent storm, depicts a ship washed entirely into the lagoon at Kure Atoll, equipment being swept off the decks as the vessel passed the reef crest. The wreck of the British whaler *Pearl*, lost at Pearl and Hermes Atoll in 1822, tells a different story. There, the ship fell apart where she grounded, the crew having wrecked in calmer conditions on the uncharted atoll. Salvage was possible, and soon a schooner named *Deliverance* was constructed on the beach.

The steam machinery and armament of the USS *Saginaw*, lost in 1870, represents a slice of Civil War history in the Pacific. The remains of the side wheel navy steamer are scattered on top and underneath the reef crest. Heavier objects, such as the cannon, steam engines, and paddlewheel shafts, are solidly embedded in the coralline substrate.

Brenda Altmeier swims above the wreckage of the Dunnottar Castle. *Photo Credit: Robert Schwemmer, NOAA.*

The capstans, anchors, masts, and rigging of the *Dunnottar Castle*, a 258-foot (79-meter) iron-hulled sailing ship lost in 1886, portray the days of the great sailing ships like the *Falls of Clyde* (now part of the Hawai'i Maritime Center), the *Balcalutha*, and the *Star of India*, a time when maritime commerce was driven by steel masts and canvas and human hands. The wreck site is an inventory of industrial wind-driven commerce long before humans' dependence on fossil fuels.

Today, Papahānaumokuākea plays a critical role in two major living traditions of Native Hawaiians: Hawaiian voyaging and wayfinding. The voyaging route between Kaua'i (in the main Hawaiian Islands) and Nihoa and Mokumanamana is used today as the best training ground for apprentices of Hawaiian wayfinding, non-instrument navigation, before undertaking a long, open ocean voyage beyond the archipelago. At Papahānaumokuākea, an array of attributes unique in the archipelago makes the area the ideal training platform for novice Hawaiian wayfinders. Apprentice navigators are challenged to sail to Nihoa from Lehua, a small, crescent shaped island near Kaua'i and Ni'ihau.

Anchor and bow section of the whaling ship Parker at Kure Atoll. *Photo credit: Tane Casserly, NOAA Office of National Marine Sanctuaries.*

Oral histories document that this navigational test was used in generations past; it is an ideal route for a novice navigator to prove new skills in reading the celestial and ocean environment. The navigator must find an island that cannot be seen on the horizon, but is still within a relatively short sail from the safety and provisions of a larger island. Today, novice Hawaiian wayfinders are considered qualified to attempt to navigate a canoe on long-distance, trans-Pacific sails after they have successfully guided a voyage from Kaua'i to Nihoa.

Hawaiian navigators sailing a multi-hulled canoe.
By: John Webber, ca 1781.

Hokule'a, The Hawaiian Voyaging Society's outrigger canoe, escorts the Ocean Futures Society expedition vessel Searcher out of the Honolulu Harbor on July 6, 2003. *Photo credit: Tom Ordway, Ocean Futures Society.*

Key Species Within the Monument

SEABIRDS

Papahānaumokuākea is home to more than 14 million birds living seasonally in what is collectively the largest tropical seabird rookery in the world. Twenty species of tropical and subtropical seabirds breed in Papahānaumokuākea. Virtually all of the world's entire populations of Laysan albatross and black-footed albatross live there, as well as populations of global significance of red-tailed tropicbirds, Bonin petrels, Tristram's storm-petrels, and white terns.

MANTA RAYS

Manta rays (hāhālua in Hawaiian) are large fish, weighing up to 3,000 lbs (1,360 kg). Their wingspan can exceed 20 feet (6 meters), and the largest manta recorded was 23 feet (7 meters). They have cartilaginous skeletons and are related to sharks. One of the defining features of these fish is their pair of "cephalic flaps" which act to funnel water into the mouth. When curled up, these flaps resemble horns pro-jecting from the head. Mantas are harmless to humans, but can be quite intimidating when seen up close due to their immense size. They prey upon tiny plankton and swoop in great looping circles with their gaping mouths open wide. Similar to humpback whale fluke

A red-footed booby perched on a dead *Tournefortia* branch.
Photo credit: Tom Ordway, Ocean Futures Society.

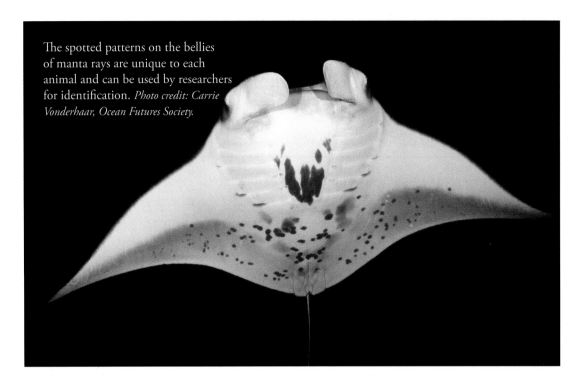

The spotted patterns on the bellies of manta rays are unique to each animal and can be used by researchers for identification. *Photo credit: Carrie Vonderhaar, Ocean Futures Society.*

patterns, mantas can be identified by the pattern of blotches and dark spots on their undersides. At one time there were thought to be several species of manta but DNA research by Tim Clark at the University of Hawai'i has shown they are all the same species.

They are the color of midnight, some with moon white bellies and mottled spots like splattered ink on satin. And seen from the deck of a ship in crystal clear water, their backs etched in chalky markings appear like dancing skeletons beneath a sheer black cloak, la manta, the origin of their Spanish name. Large wandering eyes resemble those of hammerhead sharks, allowing good vision forward and below. With a swift bank or somersault, they quickly acquire a reverse field of view. The brain to body ratio for manta rays according to scientists, is the largest for all sharks, and similar in ratio to that of marsupials and birds.

Unlike other rays, mantas have no stingers and only vestigial remnants of teeth; instead these devilfish, like giant whale sharks, are filter-feeding members of the family

Céline and Fabien Cousteau's powerful movie lights attract plankton, which the mantas feed on. *Photo credit: Carrie Vonderhaar, Ocean Futures Society.*

of sharks. When furled, their cephalic lobes look like horns, but when loosened, sweep the ocean like arms open wide to scoop plankton towards yawning mouths as they move through the sea. Brush-like gill-rakers in their mouths filter the water to capture small crustaceans and tiny bony fishes before oxygen is extracted, carbon dioxide "exhaled" and the depleted water forced back into the sea. Solo swimmers may form squadrons around zones of upwelling near underwater pinnacles, channels and drop-offs. Somersaulting in graceful loops, mantas feed in patches of plankton, consuming as much as 60 pounds (27 kg) in a day.

In Hawai'i, they are known as Hāhālua, and have earned the endearment of locals as a living tourism resource. Small populations congregate in the Northwestern Hawaiian Islands, along the coasts of Maui and the Big Island. While diving with them along the southern shore of Kilauea in view of the towering crater Halemaumau and the fiery goddess Pele, we fell spell to their beauty beneath a starry night sky.

One of the greatest thrills of being in nature is to be noticed by another aware creature. For divers, it is rare to have an animal approach, and so for Céline and Fabien Cousteau, diving with large and powerful manta rays was exhilarating, especially at night. "There were five to seven of them and you could identify them by their scars and different markings. One of the mantas that they've identified is known to come in close and she actually bumped my head a few times. It wasn't something that caused fear; if anything, it caused excitement and I couldn't wait for her to come back just to have that moment of   contact with that beautiful animal. I definitely didn't want to come back up. It never got tiring to have them come right to my face, and then go into the darkness, swim in a big circle and come back around.

Céline and Fabien Cousteau are dwarfed by a manta ray, or devilfish. *Photo credit: Carrie Vonderhaar, Ocean Futures Society.*

"The film crew on the outer edge; the mantas in the middle ring, and Fabien and me in the center—it was like a ballet within a ballet. The really impressive thing is having these big animals appear out of nowhere, and then, just as they appeared, disappear. You're left waiting for the next one. For me, there was an inner excitement and at the same time an outer calmness. To really describe it, I have to make large gestures with my arms as I talk about the manta rays swooping down on us, just barely missing my head with their wings . . . or in a few cases, scraping the top of my head with their sandpaper bellies, making my already knotty, salted hair a little more disheveled. It was magical." [Céline Cousteau]

HAWAIIAN MONK SEALS

The Hawaiian monk seal is one of the most endangered marine mammals in the world. Only about 1,100 seals are left and their population is declining. Monk seals are endemic to Hawaiʻi, meaning they are native and are not found anywhere else in the world. Hawaiian monk seals are protected under the Endangered Species Act, Marine Mammal Protection Act, and state law in Hawaiʻi. These laws prohibit harassing, harming, or killing a

Hawaiian monk seal at East Island, French Frigate Shoals. *Photo credit: Andy Collins, NOAA Office of National Marine Sanctuaries.*

Endangered Hawaiian monk seal.
Photo credit: Andy Collins, NOAA.

monk seal. In 1988, critical habitat was designated on all beach areas and ocean waters to a depth of 120 feet (37 meters) around the Northwestern Hawaiian Islands.

The monk seal is known in Hawaiian as ʻIlio-holo-i-ka-uaua, which means "dog running in the rough seas," or na mea hulu, which means "the furry one." It is Hawaiʻi's state mammal.

Hawaiian monk seals reach reproductive maturity at five or six years old. Their life expectancy is 25-30 years, but few seals live this long. These animals usually dive for an average of six minutes when feeding; but they can hold their breath as long as 20 minutes. Monk seals can dive as deep as 1,500 feet (457 meters), but they usually make dives less than 200 feet (61 meters) to forage on the sea floor.

Monk seals usually sleep on the beaches of the Hawaiian Islands, sometimes for days at a time. SCUBA divers can sometimes see them sleeping underwater in small caves. Monk seals do not migrate seasonally, but some seals have been tracked traveling hundreds of miles in the open ocean. Individual seals often frequent the same beaches over and over, but do not defend regular territories. Hawaiian monk seals do not live in colonies like sea lions or elephant seals. They are mostly solitary but sometimes may be seen lying near each other in small groups—usually not touching.

Hawaiian monk seals are "generalist" feeders, which means they eat a variety of foods depending on what's available. They eat many types of common fishes, squid, octopus, eels and crustaceans (crabs, shrimp and lobster). Diet studies indicate that they prefer prey that is easier to catch than most of the locally popular gamefish.

Adult monk seals are about 5-7 feet (1.5-2 meters) in length and weigh about 400-600 pounds (180-270 kilograms). Females are slightly larger than males. Monk seal pups are black, while adults are dark gray to brown on their back and light gray to yellowish brown on their belly. Monk seals have a "catastrophic molt," where they shed the top layer of their skin and fur about once a year. When seals spend a long time at sea foraging, they can grow algae on their fur. Seals that look green usually haven't molted recently and may be getting ready to shed into a shiny, new coat.

People who are lucky enough to see a monk seal in the wild should maintain a minimum distance of 150 feet (45 meters) to ensure the monk seal is not disturbed. A disease transferred from dogs to seals could threaten the entire monk seal population so pets must be leashed and kept away from seals. Federal permits are required to conduct research on monk seals both in the wild and in captivity.

- Report violations to the NOAA Fisheries Enforcement Hotline at 1-800-853-1964.
- Report monk seal sightings and marine mammal emergencies (including injuries and entanglements) to NOAA Fisheries at 1-888-256-9840.

Hawaiian Monk Seal on Green Island at Kure Atoll State Wildlife Refuge in the Papahānaumokuākea Marine National Monument. *Photo credit: Claire Fackler, NOAA National Marine Sanctuaries.*

Emerging Environmental Issues

MARINE DEBRIS

From fishing gear, lost or abandoned at sea, to cigarette butts and bottle caps, marine debris is an increasing problem in coastal areas worldwide and is a severe and chronic threat to wildlife and marine habitats in the Papahānaumokuākea Marine National Monument. Ocean currents carry a wide array of marine debris, including derelict fishing nets and other gear, household plastics, hazardous materials, and shore-based debris. Currents concentrate the materials and deposit them on the reefs and beaches of the island chain. Marine debris poses a threat to marine animals through entanglement (primarily in derelict fishing gear) and through ingestion of debris.

LtCDR Marc Pickett and Lt. Mark Sarmek wrestle to free an entangled Hawaiian monk seal at French Frigate Shoals during a marine debris survey and removal cruise. They were successful.
Photo credit: Ray Boland, NOAA Fisheries.

Jean-Michel Cousteau walks a litter-strewn beach on Laysan Island in the Papahānaumokuākea Marine National Monument. *Photo credit: Nancy Marr, Ocean Futures Society.*

The debris hinders the recovery of the critically endangered Hawaiian monk seal and threatens sea turtles and other marine life through entanglement, drowning and suffocation hazards. Between 1982 and 2003 there were 238 documented monk seal entanglements in marine debris in the Northwestern Hawaiian Islands, though many more likely occurred. In addition, debris frequently entangles and kills corals, leads to the death of seabirds through entanglement in nets and accidental consumption of floating plastics, and poses a navigation hazard. A successful multi-agency effort has removed more than 770 tons (700 metric tons) of debris from Papahānaumokuākea reefs in the past ten years.

Birds are also harmed by debris. Smaller types of marine debris made of plastic, such as disposable lighters, bottle caps, and other fragments, are ingested by adult albatrosses, shearwaters, and other seabirds when they feed at sea. These objects are subsequently fed to chicks and can cause direct and indirect injuries, often resulting in the death of young albatrosses. Additionally, this debris may increase the birds' exposure to and ingestion of organochlorine contaminants from plastic surfaces.

After searching for miles across the vast Pacific for food, a black-footed albatross feeds its hungry chick a meal. While the meal contains nutritious fish eggs and squid, it also unfortunately includes plastic, picked up by the adult bird in the foraging process. *Photo credit: Tove Petterson, Ocean Futures Society.*

A Laysan albatross, dead from ingested plastic, on Midway Island,
Northwestern Hawaiian Islands Marine National Monument.
Photo credit: Holly Lohuis, Ocean Futures Society.

Non-native invertebrates like this Christmas-tree hydroid have become established in the Northwestern Hawaiian Islands.
Photo credit: Exculapio.

ALIEN AND INVASIVE SPECIES

Invasive species are causing significant ecological and economic impacts worldwide. An invasive species is defined as a non-native (or alien) species whose introduction causes or is likely to cause economic or environmental harm or harm to human health. It is nearly impossible to determine which alien species will become invasive and have harmful impacts on an ecosystem. Therefore, a precautionary approach treats all alien species as potentially invasive. While only nineteen alien species have been detected in the waters of Papahānaumokuākea, global trends suggest that the threat is high. Alien species may be introduced accidentally, such as with vessel discharge, marine debris, or aquaculture, or intentionally, as in the case of a few species of snappers, grouper and algae. Once established, invasive species can be extremely costly to control and would likely be impossible to eradicate from reefs. On land, several invasive species have already dramatically damaged ecosystems. Requirements to wear new, previously frozen clothes when visiting sensitive land areas, and treating diving equipment in a dilute bleach solution help to prevent new introductions.

- **Frozen Clothes:** The tiny land areas of the NWHI have been isolated from each other for millions of years, and they have developed unique plant and animal communities. Although the main Hawaiian Islands have been overrun by non-natives, islands such as Nihoa preserve the last remaining examples of intact Hawaiian coastal plant communities. For this very reason it is necessary for visitors to wear new clothes that have been previously frozen for 48 hours, stored in sealed bags and worn only just prior to landing. The freezing kills insect hitchhikers, and may sterilize plant seeds. Such precautionary measures help to maintain these fragile habitats, and prevent introduction of new species by human transport. Visitors to sensitive land areas in Papahānaumokuākea must plan accordingly to have separate sets of frozen gear for each area they visit.

- **Bleaching Scuba Gear:** When diving or snorkeling, people can unknowingly pick up pieces of algae and other living matter on their gear. Some species of algae can stay alive for days, or even weeks out of the water unless thoroughly dried, and can be transported from one area to another. Certain species that grow quickly can be aggressive invaders, and can displace native algae. Soaking dive gear in a dilute bleach solution (about 1/8 cup bleach/gallon water—7.5 ml/liter water) between dive locations can help prevent transporting invasive algae, coral disease pathogens and other critters to areas where they are not currently found. In the Papahānaumokuākea Marine National Monument, divers must soak their dive gear for 24 hours in fresh water prior to entering the area and treat their dive equipment between dive locations with the bleach solution. Visual inspections of gear for algal fragments are also required.

- **Clean Boat Hulls of Hitchhikers:** Most mariners know that if they leave their boat in the water for a while algae, barnacles and other invertebrates will eventually start growing on it. When boating around home this is not an issue, except to slow the boat down, but when traveling to new areas, especially sensitive areas like Papahānaumokuākea Marine National Monument, this can be a real problem. Boats may be transporting hitchhikers that detach or fall off in the new area and start reproducing, possibly displacing native species. Hull inspection and cleaning before entering sensitive or new areas helps to prevent unknowingly spreading plants or animals to areas where they may cause harm. Permitted vessels must inspect their hulls and clean them, if necessary, prior to entering the monument.

Research Within the Monument

The Papahānaumokuākea Marine National Monument consists of a complex assemblage of natural resources in relatively undisturbed condition compared with the main Hawaiian Islands and many other marine-based ecosystems in the world. Protecting the health and integrity of these resources is a key priority for resource managers. Scientific, cultural and maritime research are important parts of the overall operations of the Monument. Research projects within the Monument include:

- **What is out there and how can we conserve it?** The Monument's coral reef research program focuses on basic habitat characterization. Reef surveys have recorded the diversity and abundance of fishes, algae, corals, and other reef invertebrates at numerous locations throughout the archipelago. In 2010, divers used specialized equipment to descend as far as 250 feet (76 meters) underwater, finding several new species and high concentrations of fish found nowhere else in the world. From October 1 – 14, 2011, Papahānaumokuākea Marine National Monument's intertidal monitoring expedition completed the third consecutive year of research and monitoring activities along shallow, wave-swept, rocky shorelines of Nihoa, Mokumanamana, French Frigate Shoals and Gardner Pinnacles in the Northwestern Hawaiian Islands.

- **Movement of Big Predators.** Top predators, such as sharks, jacks and groupers, play an important role in marine ecosystems. By feeding on other organisms, they help to keep the entire ecosystem in balance. Science-based management and protection requires an understanding of the movement patterns of top predators. Researchers tag sharks and other big fish in order to learn about movement patterns in the Hawaiian Archipelago. These tags can relay information on the shark's position to underwater listening stations or to satellites orbiting hundreds of miles above the Earth. So far, research has shown that the animals are wide-ranging within the atolls and at least two species move between atolls, crossing the open ocean. One tagged tiger shark traveled from French Frigate Shoals to Kona—700 miles (1,125 km) away. Another traveled from French Frigate Shoals to Midway (about 1,300 miles/2,100 km). Clear patterns of movement have also begun to emerge. Ulua (giant trevally) display regular day/night movements, as well as seasonal movement patterns based on the phases of the moon.

- **Artifact Conservation/ New Life for Old.** Maritime archaeologists do not remove artifacts from a wreck site until the entire site has been properly surveyed and documented. Artifacts may be recovered if there is a chance that the site may be subject to looting or damage. Also, artifact recovery may be important for further research, education and outreach, and identification of a site. Experts with a great deal of experience conserving artifacts submerged for hundreds of years in seawater are able to reverse some of the processes of degradation that occur on the sea-floor. Since shipwreck sites in the Northwestern Hawaiian Islands are remote, few people will ever get to visit them. Exhibits such as the "Lost on a Reef" exhibit at Mokupāpapa Discovery Center in Hilo help visitors to get a chance to understand these sites and connect with pieces of this history. The artifacts are a window into the broader story of maritime heritage in the Monument.

Opening of Lost on a Reef exhibit at Mokupāpapa including conserved artifacts from Papahānaumokuākea Marine National Monument. *Photo credit: NOAA/Collins.*

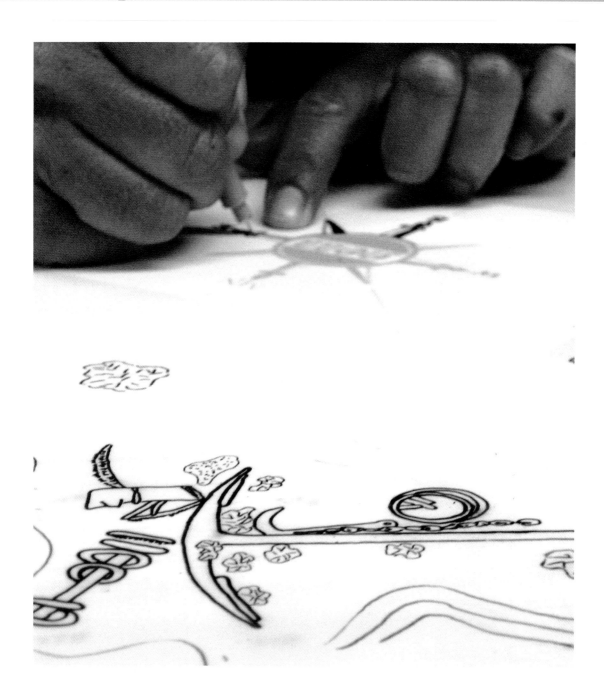

A maritime archaeologist mapping a shipwreck site in the Papahānaumokuākea Marine National Monument. *Photo credit: Paulo Maurin.*

Visiting the Monument

Note: In the last section of the book, "When You Visit the Sanctuaries," is detailed information about resources found within each sanctuary/monument to help visitors have an enjoyable and productive visit.

VISITOR'S CENTER

Mokupāpapa Discovery Center   Open Tuesday - Saturday 9 a.m. - 4 p.m.
76 Kamehameha Ave   (Closed on federal holidays)
Hilo, Hawai'i 96720   **Admission is free**
                                        Telephone: 808-933-8181

In May of 2003, the Mokupāpapa Discovery Center opened on the bayfront in Hilo, Hawai'i. This 4,000 square foot facility was constructed to interpret the natural science, culture, and history of the Northwestern Hawaiian Islands and surrounding marine environment. Interactive displays, engaging three-dimensional models, and immersive theater allow the visitor to experience the wonder and majesty of this special ocean region. A 2,500-gallon (9,400-liter) salt-water aquarium provides a habitat for some of the fishes from the region's reefs. Next to the aquarium, in a small alcove is a mock-up of Hawai'i Undersea Research Laboratory's *Pisces V* submersible. Using working robot arms, visitors can experience what it might be like as a researcher descending into the dark depths of the ocean.

Large and colorful graphic panels with interpretive text in both Hawaiian and English introduce the visitor to the NWHI, its geography, cultural history, and ecology. Beautiful photographs from the NWHI are spread throughout the Center and a giant coral reef mural created by Hilo artist Layne Luna covers an entire wall in the main exhibit hall. Layne also created several life-size models of NWHI inhabitants that hang from the ceiling and hide in corners. A giant manta ray swoops down over the entry door as tiger and Galapagos sharks prowl overhead. A large Ulua (giant trevally) swims out of the coral reef mural to feed on Akule (big-eyed scad) and in the program room two large Ahi (yellowfin tuna) explode out of a wall to bite traditional Hawaiian lures being towed behind the double-

Exhibits in the Mokupāpapa Discovery Center.
Photo credit: Papahānaumokuākea Marine National Monument.

hulled canoe. The abundant natural life of the NWHI comes alive within the center and the visitor is transported into this remote ocean wilderness where predators still rule the reefs and the skies teem with seabirds.

As the visitor leaves the main exhibit hall they leave the marine environment and enter the sparse land areas of the NWHI where the skies are filled with millions of swooping, screeching birds. Every year millions of seabirds return to these small islands to breed. A lava bench extends from one wall and acts as a mini-theater for people to watch and listen to the Kumulipo, the Hawaiian creation chant, set to images and video. Seabirds swirl overhead, casting their shadows on the walls. A pile of marine debris reaches to the ceiling and introduces how marine debris is a major environmental threat in the NWHI where it entangles marine life and breaks fragile corals. An exhibit explains the scope of the problem and what NOAA and other partners are doing to address this issue.

Throughout the center, multimedia exhibits in video kiosks and on plasma screens invite visitors to explore the NWHI at their own pace and in their own way. Video kiosks present the world of the coral reef researcher, as well as the conservationist, and a virtual field guide entices visitors to identify the many different plants and animals that inhabit the NWHI.

A large Ulua, or giant trevally, swims out of the coral reef mural to feed on Akule, or big-eyed scad. *Photo credit: Papahānaumokuākea Marine National Monument.*

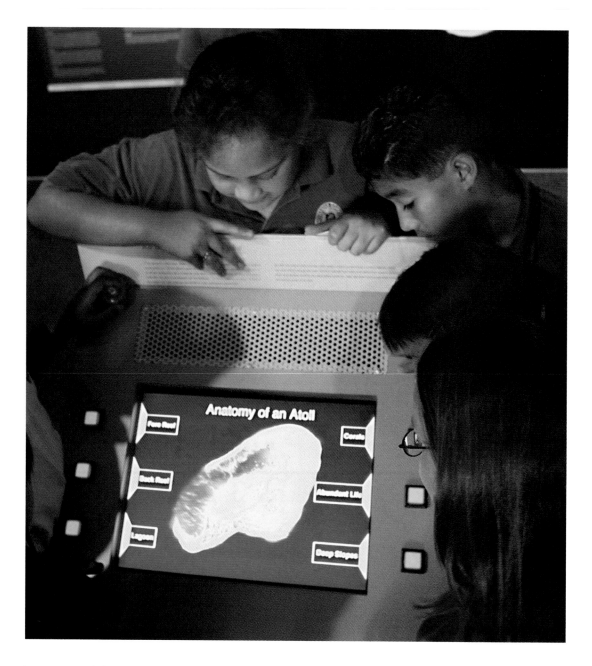

Interactive exhibits are throughout the Mokupāpapa Discovery Center.
Photo credit: Papahānaumokuākea Marine National Monument.

Regional office locations
Main Office:
1845 Wasp Blvd, Building 176
Honolulu, HI 96818
Telephone: 808-725-5800

The Midway Atoll National Wildlife Refuge and Battle of Midway National Memorial is the only location within the Papahānaumokuākea Marine National Monument that is open to the public. All activities at Midway require a Monument permit. Numerous provisions of the permit ensure the protection of Midway's wildlife and historic resources while allowing visitors to learn about and experience this unique ecosystem. It may be possible for individuals to make reservations to visit the Monument with permitted companies.[9] Permits will be considered for recreational activities that do not involve fee-for-service transactions (noncommercial) and occur only within the Midway Atoll Special Management area. Recreational activities are defined as, "an activity conducted for personal enjoyment that does not result in the extraction of monument resources and that does not involve a fee-for-service transaction. This includes, but is not limited to, wildlife viewing, SCUBA diving, snorkeling, and boating." Permit applications and instructions can be downloaded from the Monument website.[10] Permits must be requested at least four to six months in advance.[11]

---

9   http://www.papahanaumokuakea.gov/midway/welcome.html
10   http://www.papahanaumokuakea.gov/resource/permits.html
11   http://www.papahanaumokuakea.gov/resource/support/permit_brochure_aug_2010.pdf

BOATING

All applicants planning to access Papahānaumokuākea via vessel must request a permit and must complete the following Monument vessel requirements prior to permit issuance: hull inspection, rat inspection and installation of a Monument-approved Vessel Monitoring System. Anchoring on coral is prohibited.

Unpermitted vessels may pass through the monument without interruption provided that they notify the Monument prior to entering and after leaving the Monument.[12]

All vessels conducting activities within the Monument must have a valid Monument permit.
Photo credit: Tom Ordway, Ocean Futures Society.

---

12   http://www.papahanaumokuakea.gov/resource/ship_reporting.html

> **To notify the Monument of passage call: toll-free in the U.S.: (866)478-NWHI (6944), or outside the U.S., via satellite phone, or on Oʻahu: (808)395-NWHI (6944), or send an email to nwhi.notifications@noaa.gov.**

Vessels will be asked to provide the following information: position, vessel identification, contact information of owner and operator, USCG documentation, state license or registration number, home port, intended and actual route through the monument, categories of hazardous cargo, length of vessel, and propulsion type. Additional restrictions apply to National Wildlife Refuges, the State Northwestern Hawaiian Islands Marine Refuge and Kure Atoll State Wildlife Sanctuary.

FISHING

Sustenance fishing only is allowed within the Midway Atoll Special Management Area. Restrictions apply.[13] Fishing is not allowed in other areas of the Papahānaumokuākea Marine National Monument.

DIVING/SNORKELING

Snorkeling and SCUBA diving requires a permit[14] and is limited to the Midway Atoll Special Management Area.

Jean-Michel Cousteau's expedition team enjoys its reward of a great dive on Rapture Reef, which boasts beautiful 100-foot visibility and schools of jacks.
Photo credit: Tom Ordway, Ocean Futures Society.

---

13   http://www.papahanaumokuakea.gov/resource/support/sustenance_fishing_policy_final.pdf
14   http://www.papahanaumokuakea.gov/resource/permits.html

When You Visit the Sanctuaries

Hawaiian Islands Humpback Whale National Marine Sanctuary

Sanctuary Office and Visitor Center

Hawaiian Islands Humpback Whale National Marine Sanctuary
726 South Kīhei Road
Kīhei, HI 96753
Telephone: 808-879-2818
Toll Free: 800-831-4888
Fax: 808-874-3815
Email: hihumpbackwhale@noaa.gov
hawaiihumpbackwhale.noaa.gov/welcome.html

Visitor Center Hours: Monday – Friday, 10 a.m. – 3 p.m.
Free Admission

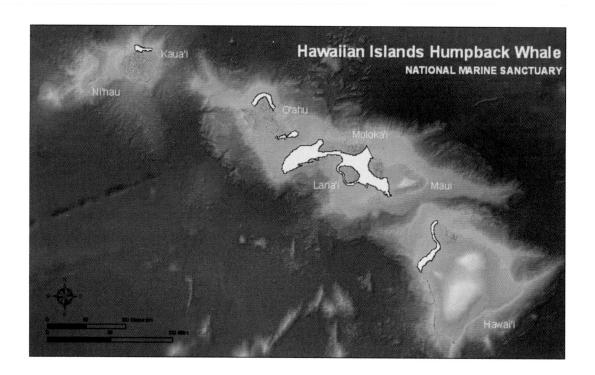

Chamber of Commerce

Maui Chamber of Commerce
The J. Walter Cameron Center
95 Mahalani St, Suite #22A
Wailuku, HI 96793
Telephone: 808-244-0081
Fax: 808-244-0083
Email: office@mauichamber.com
www.mauichamber.com

Air & Ground Transportation

Aircraft Services

Maui International Airport (Kahului Airport) (OGG, www.hawaii.gov/ogg) is the primary airport on the island of Maui and receives both overseas and inter-island flights. Major international carriers and several commuter airlines serve Maui: Air Canada, Aloha Airlines, American Airlines, American Trans Air, America West, Continental Airlines, Delta Airlines, Harmony Airlines, Hawaiian Airlines, Island Air, Northwest Airlines, Pacific Wings Airlines, United Airlines, West Jet Airlines.

1 Kahului Airport Road
Kahului, HI 96732
Telephone: 808-872-3830

Rental Cars

Rental car agencies at the airport include:

Alamo Rent-A-Car
Telephone: 808-872-1470
Toll Free: 800-327-9633

Avis Rent-A-Car
Telephone: 808-871-7576
Toll Free: 800-321-3712

Budget Rent-A-Car
Telephone: 808-871-8811
Toll Free: 800-527-7000

Dollar Rent-A-Car
Telephone: 808-877-2732
Toll Free: 800-800-4000

Enterprise Rent-A-Car
Telephone: 808-871-1511
Toll Free: 800-736-8222

Hertz Rent-A-Car
Telephone: 808-893-5200
Toll Free: 800-654-3131

National Rent-A-Car
Telephone: 808-871-8852
Toll Free: 888-826-6890

Thrifty Rent-A-Car
Telephone: 808-877-2732
Toll Free: 800-847-4389

Taxi/Shuttle

Kahului Airport Taxi Service is managed by Robert's Tours & Transportation, Inc., 808-877-0907.

Shuttle Service offering one way and roundtrip services is provided by Roberts Hawaii. The Maui Airport Shuttle Service counter is located in the Baggage Claim area. No reservations are needed.

Contact Roberts Hawaii for specific rates to your destination.
Telephone: 808-954-8630
Toll Free: 866-293-1782
Email: CustomerService@RobertsHawaii.com
www.airportmauishuttle.com

Accommodations, Restaurants, Markets and Attractions

Because of the wide variety of commercial enterprises available to the public, we recommend that visitors check with area Chambers of Commerce for lists of local businesses in all categories, from where to stay to where to eat and what to do.

Diving/Snorkeling

Some of the many dive and snorkeling shops near the Sanctuary are:

The Scuba Shack
2349 S Kīhei Rd
Kīhei, HI 96753
Telephone: 808-891-0500
www.scubashack.com

Maui Dive Shop
1455 S Kīhei Rd., Ste 1
Kīhei, HI, 96753
Telephone: 808-879-3388
www.mauidiveshop.com

Maui Diving Scuba Center Snorkel Shop
222 Papalaua St., Ste 112
Lahaina, HI, 96761
Toll Free: 800-959-7319

Extended Horizons Scuba
94 Kupuohi St., Ste A1
Lahaina, HI, 96761
Telephone: 808-667-0611
www.extendedhorizons.com

Boating

Some of the many boating companies near the Sanctuary are:

> Seaescape Boat Rentals
> 165 Halekuai St.
> Kīhei, HI, 96753
> Telephone: 808-879-3721
> www.maui-boat-rental.com

> Wailea Boating Company, Ltd.
> 1280 S Kīhei Rd., Ste 225
> Kīhei, HI 96753
> Telephone: 808-891-2628
> www.waileaboatingcompany.com

> Maui Boat Trips
> 50 Puu Hale St.
> Lahaina, HI 96761
> Toll Free: 800-490-0849
> www.mauiboattrips.com

Fishing

Some of the many fishing charter companies near the Sanctuary are:
> Local Fishing Knowledge Day Tours
> 1215 S Kīhei Rd.
> Kīhei, HI 96753
> Telephone: 808-385-1337
> www.localfishingknowledge.com

Maui Shore Fishing Guides
3740 Lower Honoapiilani Rd., Apt A206
Lahaina, HI 96761
Telephone: 808-344-1724
www.mauishorefishingguides.com

Maui Fish Company
1275 Haiku Rd
Haiku, HI 96708
Telephone: 808-575-9118
www.mauifish.net

Whale Watching

Some of the whale watching companies near the Sanctuary are:

Ultimate Whale Watch
17 Lahaina Harbor
Lahaina, HI 96761
Telephone: 808-667-5678
www.ultimatewhalewatch.com

Pacific Whale Foundation - Whalewatch Lahaina
612 Front St.
Lahaina, HI 96761
Telephone: 808-249-8811
www.pacificwhale.org

Kayak Rental

Some of the kayak rental companies near the Sanctuary are:

Maui Kayaks
505 Front St., Ste 140
Lahaina, HI 96761
Telephone: 808-874-4000
www.mauikayaks.com

Kelii's Kayak Tours
158 Lanakila Place
Kīhei, HI 96753
Telephone: 808-874-7652
www.keliiskayak.com

South Pacific Kayak
95 Halekuai St.
Kīhei, HI 96753
Telephone: 808-875-4848
www.southpacifickayaks.com

Aloha Kayaks Maui
155 Halekuai St.
Kīhei, HI 96753
Telephone: 808-270-3318
www.alohakayaksmaui.com

Remember, if you cannot find what you are looking for on these pages, contact the local area Chamber of Commerce for help. Even if they don't know the answer to your question, they will find it for you. Enjoy your Sanctuary visit.

National Marine Sanctuary of American Samoa

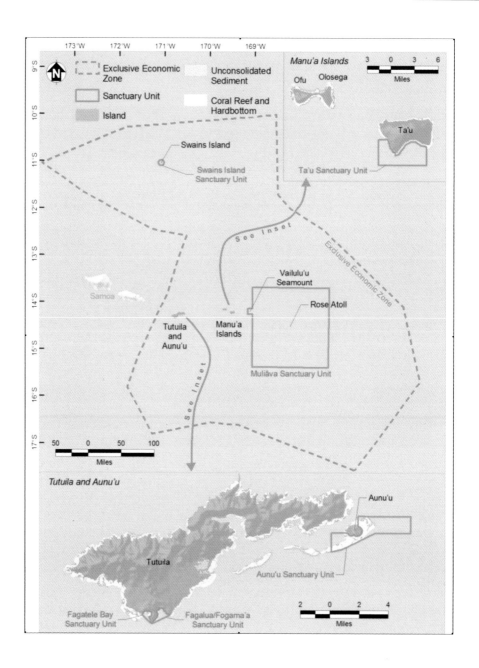

Regional Office

National Marine Sanctuary of American Samoa
P.O. Box 4318
Pago Pago, American Samoa 96799
Telephone: 684-633-6500
Fax: 684-633-6511
Email: fagatelebay@noaa.gov
http://americansamoa.noaa.gov/welcome.html

Tauese P.F. Sunia Ocean Center
Fagtogo, Pago Pago
Tutuila 96799
Telephone: 683-633-6500
Visitor Hours: Monday – Friday, 9 a.m. – 4 p.m.
                        Saturday, 9 a.m. – 12 noon

Because of its remote location and geographic makeup (six protected areas, covering 13,581 square miles of nearshore coral reef and offshore open ocean waters across the Samoan Archipelago) visiting this Sanctuary requires significant advance planning. American Samoa is located in the Pacific Ocean, more than half way between Hawaii and New Zealand. Visitors from the United States can travel directly from Honolulu, Hawaii.

All visitors to American Samoa require a valid passport, a return ticket or onward ticket, and sufficient funds to support their stay. US Citizens and US Nationals do not require a visa and may enter and leave freely.

Visitors are welcome to explore the sanctuary. Please visit the National Marine Sanctuary of American Samoa website or come to the Ocean Center for a tour and receive a map of the trail leading to Fagatele Bay. It is suggested to call the Marine Sanctuary staff a day in advance at 684-633-6500 so arrangements can be made.

Chamber of Commerce

We were unable to identify information about an American Samoa Chamber of Commerce. Therefore, we provide below an excellent alternative for local information.

American Samoa Visitors Bureau
PO Box 4240
Pago Pago AS 96799
American Samoa

Suite 200, Fagaima Center One
Corner Airport & Fagaima Roads
Tafuna, American Samoa
Telephone: 684-699-9805
Fax: 684-699-9806
Email: info@americansamoa.travel

Air & Ground Transportation

Aircraft Services

Pago Pago Airport (PPG)
American Samoa
PO Box 1539
Pago Pago 96799, American Samoa
Telephone: 684-699-9101
Fax: 684-699-4039
email: tsf_6@yahoo.com

There are limited flights from the United States to Pago Pago. Hawaiian Airlines offers flights from Honolulu and Los Angeles. Flights between the Samoan islands are offered by Inter Island Airways.

Hawaiian Airlines
Toll Free: 800-367-5320
www.hawaiianairlines.com

Inter Island Airways, Incorporated
Pago Pago International Airport
4929 Airport Road, Hangar 2
P.O. Box 4929
Pago Pago, American Samoa 96799 USA
Telephone: 684-699-7100
www.interislandair.com

Rental Cars

Avis Rental Cars
Telephone: 684-699-2746
Email: rthompson@asco.as

Dollar Car Rentals
Telephone: 684-699-1179
Email: dollar@samoatelco.com

Latone's Car Rental
Telephone: 684-633-5005
Email: tones@samoatelco.com

Lupelele Rentals
Telephone: 684-699-5898

Sadie's Rental Cars
Telephone: 684-633-5900

Sir Amos Car Rental
Telephone: 684-699-4554
Email: siramosrental@yahoo.com

Tautai Rentals:
Telephone: 684-699-5294
Email: reservations@tautaicarrentals.as

Taxis

Airport Cab
Telephone: 684-699-1800

Airport Taxi Association
Telephone: 684-699-4242

Airport Taxi Service
Telephone: 684-699-1169

Roses Taxi Stand
Telephone: 684-699-1136

Fishing/Diving/Snorkeling

Pago Pago Marine Charters
PO Box 1215, Pago Pago
American Samoa 96799
Telephone: 684-699-9234
Cell: 684-733-0964

Fax: 684-699-9136
pagocharters@gmail.com
www.pagopagomarinecharters.com

Yacht Charter Neverland
Ferdinand Pohl
Email: ferdinandpohl@hotmail.com
www.catamaran-yacht-charters.com

At the time of printing, there is no Chamber of Commerce office operating in American Samoa. For additional information, you may want to contact travel agencies doing business in American Samoa.

Papahānaumokuākea Marine National Monument

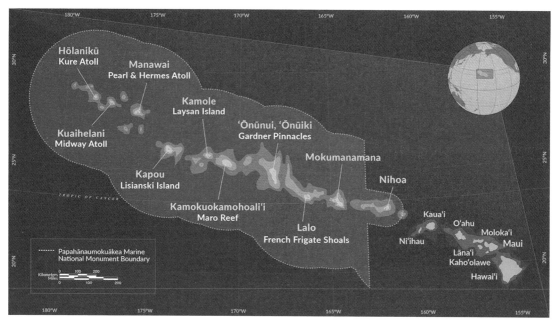

Photo credit: NOAA - http://www.papahanaumokuakea.gov/

Main Office

The Papahānaumokuākea Marine National Monument main office has relocated to historic Ford Island on Oʻahu.

NOAA/Daniel K. Inouye Regional Center
NOS/ONMS/PMNM
1845 Wasp Blvd, Building 176
Honolulu, HI 96818
Telephone: 808-725-5800
Fax: 808-455-3093
Email: hawaiireef@noaa.gov

For more information about the Monument, contact:

Mokupāpapa Discovery Center
76 Kamehameha Avenue
Hilo, HI 96720
Telephone: 808-935-8358

Access to Papahānaumokuākea Marine National Monument is severely restricted to protect the pristine nature of the area. As such, public visits are not allowed. However, there are limited ways to access the Monument for specific purposes, such as to conduct cultural practices and research, habitat restoration and scientific work, and to develop educational and media products.

The following activities are <u>prohibited</u> in Papahānaumokuākea:

- Exploring for, developing, or producing oil, gas, or minerals within the Monument;
- Using or attempting to use poisons, electrical charges, or explosives in the collection or harvest of a Monument resource;
- Introducing or otherwise releasing an introduced species from within or into the Monument; and
- Anchoring on or having a vessel anchored on any living or dead coral with an anchor, anchor chain, or anchor rope.

The following activities are <u>exempted</u> from Papahānaumokuākea's permitting program:

- Response to emergencies threatening life, property, or the environment;
- Law Enforcement activities;
- Activities and exercises of the Armed Forces (including the United States Coast Guard);
- Passage without interruption.

The following activities are <u>regulated</u> through the Monument's permitting process:

- Further the understanding of Monument resources and qualities through research;
- Further the educational value of the Monument;
- Assist in the conservation and management of the Monument;
- Allow Native Hawaiian practices;
- Allow a special ocean use;
- Allow recreational activities within the Midway Atoll Special Management Area.

For assistance with the permitting process, contact:

Monument Permit Coordinator
Papahānaumokuākea Marine National Monument
NOAA/IRC, NOS/ONMS/PMNM/Permit Coordinator
1845 Wasp Blvd, Building 176
Honolulu, HI 96818
Telephone: 808-725-5800
Email: nwhipermit@noaa.gov

Because of the unique nature of this Monument, there are no listings for the infrastructure associated with a visit. Access for authorized activity is arranged through the Monument Permit Coordinator above.

Céline Cousteau eye to eye with a small cleaner shrimp in the Hawaiian Islands Humpback Whale National Marine Sanctuary. *Photo credit: Carrie Vonderhaar, Ocean Futures Society.*

A brown noddy enjoying a day at the beach on Tern Island, French Frigate Shoals. *Photo credit: Tove Petterson, Ocean Futures Society.*

An endangered green sea turtle being cleaned by a reef fish in the Hawaiian Islands Humpback Whale National Marine Sanctuary. *Photo credit: Carrie Vonderhaar, Ocean Futures Society.*

Jean-Michel Cousteau displays an array of plastic cigarette lighters, toys, vials, and other marine debris he collected during an inspection of the beach on remote Laysan Island. The debris is brought to the island by albatross, which ingest plastic litter while foraging for food at sea. These birds and their chicks may regurgitate this litter. Many times, however, the debris remains inside their gut cavities, causing death by starvation. As dead albatross decompose, these plastics are rereleased into the food chain, continuing the cycle of death from marine debris. *Photo credit: Nan Marr, Ocean Futures Society.*

Acknowledgments

- The *Explore the National Marine Sanctuaries with Jean-Michel Cousteau* series would not be possible without the creation of the two-hour PBS television special, *America's Underwater Treasures,* co-produced with KQED Public Broadcasting in San Francisco, the companion limited edition book *America's Underwater Treasures*, and the talented people who contributed to those projects
- Julie Robinson, co-author *America's Underwater Treasures* Limited Edition Book
- The staff at Ocean Futures Society: Charles Vinick, Sandra Squires, Lida Pardisi, Laura Brands, Carey Batha, Jim Knowlton, Brian Hall, Nathan Dembeck, Matthew Ferraro, Carrie Vonderhaar, Nancy Marr, Marie-Claude Oren
- Ocean Futures Society's Dr. Richard Murphy, Director of Science and Education; Pam Stacey, Co-Producer and writer of the film *America's Underwater Treasures*; Don Santee, Chief of Expeditions, and Holly Lohuis, Expedition Biologist for reviewing and fact checking the manuscript
- All of the members of the *America's Underwater Treasures* expedition team for sharing their stories and allowing us to explore the sanctuaries through their eyes
- Dr. Sylvia Earle for her Foreword
- Fabien and Céline Cousteau
- Dr. Kathryn D. Sullivan, Administrator, National Oceanic and Atmospheric Administration

- Dr. Jane Lubchenco, former Administrator, National Oceanic and Atmospheric Administration
- Daniel Basta, Director, National Marine Sanctuary System, NOAA
- Matt Stout, Communications Director, National Oceanic and Atmospheric Administration
- Sarah Marquis, West Coast/Pacific Media Coordinator, National Marine Sanctuary System, NOAA
- Allen Tom, Regional Director, Pacific Islands Region, National Marine Sanctuaries
- National Marine Sanctuary Superintendents, especially Malia Chow (Hawaiian Islands Humpback Whale) and Gene Brighouse (American Samoa)
- National Marine Sanctuary Staff and Volunteers
- National Marine Sanctuary Foundation, Jason Patlis, President, and Lori Arguelles, Past-President
- Dr. Maia McGuire, Research Editor and Compiler
- Nate Myers, Cover Designs and Interior Layouts

- And a special "Thank You" to Carrie Vonderhaar from the Ocean Publishing Team for her incredible assistance and coordination. She is absolutely terrific!

Glossary

Aquaculture: the cultivation of aquatic organisms (as fish or shellfish) especially for food

Archipelago: a group of islands

Baleen: a tough, horny material growing in comb-like fringes from the upper jaws of some species of whales; a horny keratinous substance found in two rows of transverse plates which hang down from the upper jaws of baleen whales

Basalt: a dark gray to black dense to fine-grained igneous rock

Breach (whale): to leap out of the water

Capstan: Mechanical device used chiefly on board ships or in shipyards for moving heavy weights by means of ropes, cables, or chains. A capstan consists of a drum, driven either manually or by steam or electricity, that rotates about a vertical axis to wind in a line wrapped around it

Crustacean: any of a large class of mostly water-dwelling arthropods (as lobsters, shrimps, crabs, wood lice, water fleas, and barnacles) having an exoskeleton of chitin or chitin and a compound of calcium

Echinoderm: any of a phylum of marine invertebrate animals (as starfishes, sea urchins, and sea cucumbers) that have a number of similar body parts (as the arms of a starfish) arranged around a central axis, a calcium-containing inner skeleton, and a water-vascular system

Endangered: a species that is threatened with extinction

Endangered Species Act: The federal Endangered Species Act of 1973 (ESA) (16 U.S.C.A. §§ 1531 et seq.) was enacted to protect animal and plant species from extinction by preserving the ecosystems in which they survive and by providing programs for their conservation.

Endemic: an organism that is restricted or peculiar to a locality or region

Fluke: one of the lobes of a whale's tail

Guano: excrement especially of seabirds or bats

Invertebrate: an animal without a backbone.

Krill: Any member of the crustacean suborder Euphausiacea, comprising shrimplike animals that live in the open sea

Lava tube: Lava tubes are natural conduits through which lava travels beneath the surface of a lava flow. They can be actively draining lava from a source, or can be extinct, meaning the lava flow has ceased and the rock has cooled and left a long, cave-like channel.

Leviathan: a large sea animal

Marine Mammal Protection Act: The Marine Mammal Protection Act (MMPA) of 1972 was the first article of legislation to call specifically for an ecosystem approach to natural resource management and conservation. MMPA prohibits the taking of marine mammals, and enacts a moratorium on the import, export, and sale of any marine mammal, along with any marine mammal part or product within the United States.

Mollusk: any of a large phylum (Mollusca) of invertebrate animals (as snails, clams, or squids) with a soft unsegmented body usually enclosed in a calcareous shell

Molt: to shed hair, feathers, shell, horns, or an outer layer periodically

Rebreather: an apparatus with face mask and gas supply forming a closed system from which one can breathe as long as the concentrations of oxygen and carbon dioxide remain within tolerable limits

Threatened: having an uncertain chance of continued survival; *specifically:* likely to become an endangered species

Biographies

Jean-Michel Cousteau

Explorer. Environmentalist. Educator. Film Producer. For half a century, Jean-Michel Cousteau has dedicated himself and his vast experience to communicate to people of all nations and generations his love and concern for our water planet.

Since first being "thrown overboard" by his father at the age of seven with newly invented SCUBA gear on his back, Jean-Michel has been exploring the ocean realm. The son of ocean explorer Jacques Cousteau, Jean-Michel has investigated the world's oceans aboard *Calypso* and *Alcyone* for much of his life. Honoring his heritage, Jean-Michel founded Ocean Futures Society in 1999 to carry on this pioneering work.

Ocean Futures Society, a non-profit marine conservation and education organization, serves as a "Voice for the Ocean" by communicating in all media the critical bond between people and the sea and the importance of wise environmental policy. As Ocean Futures' spokesman, Jean-Michel serves as an impassioned diplomat for the environment, reaching out to the public through a variety of media.

Jean-Michel has received many awards, including the Emmy, the Peabody Award, the 7 d'Or, and the Cable Ace Award, and has produced over 80 films. Cousteau is the executive producer of the highly acclaimed PBS television series *Jean-Michel Cousteau: Ocean Adventures*. In 2006, more than three million Americans learned about the Sanctuaries for the first time from the award-winning film *America's Underwater Treasures*, part of the *Ocean Adventures* series. Also in 2006, Jean-Michel's initiative to protect the Northwest Hawaiian Islands took him to the White House where he screened, *Voyage to Kure*, for President George W. Bush. The President was inspired and in June 2006, he declared the 1,200-mile chain of islands a Marine National Monument—at the time; the largest marine protected area in the world.

Jean-Michel is also one of the founders of the National Marine Sanctuary Foundation and is currently a Trustee Emeritus.

Most recently, Jean-Michel and his Ocean Futures Society team were among the first to survey and film under water at the Gulf of Mexico Deep Horizon oil spill. Their footage was used as evidence that large masses of oil and dispersant were traveling under water.

The mission of Ocean Futures Society is to explore our global ocean, inspiring and educating people throughout the world to act responsibly for its protection, documenting the critical connection between humanity and nature, and celebrating the ocean's vital importance to the survival of all life on our planet.

"Protect the ocean and you protect yourself"

JEAN-MICHEL COUSTEAU'S
OCEAN
FUTURES
SOCIETY

WWW.OCEANFUTURES.ORG

Ocean Futures Society is a non-profit 501(c) (3) organization, U.S. tax ID #95-4455199

Dr. Sylvia A. Earle

Dr. Sylvia A. Earle is a longtime friend of Jean-Michel Cousteau and has been a member of the Ocean Futures Society Advisory Board since its beginning in 1999. She is a pioneer in ocean exploration and research and is currently an Explorer-in-Residence at the National Geographic Society, leader of the Sustainable Seas Expeditions, chair of the Advisory Councils for Harte Research Institute and for the Ocean in Google Earth. Dr. Earle also served as Chief Scientist of NOAA in the early 1990s and she is a 2009 recipient of the coveted TED Prize for her proposal to establish a global network of Marine Protected Areas. Dr. Earle is one of the founders of the National Marine Sanctuary Foundation and is currently a Trustee Emeritus.

Photo credit: Carrie Vonderhaar, Ocean Futures Society

Dr. Maia McGuire

Born and raised in Bermuda, Dr. Maia McGuire, Research Editor and Compiler for this book, has been the University of Florida Sea Grant Extension Agent for northeast Florida since 2001. She holds a BS in Marine Biology and a PhD in Marine Biology and Fisheries. Prior related experience was with Harbor Branch Oceanographic Institution. Dr. McGuire is an active member in several organizations, including the National Marine Educators Association, Florida Marine Science Education Association, and the Association of Natural Resource Education Professionals, among others. She has won several honors and frequently speaks at regional and national conferences.

Photo credit: Debbie Penrose, Florida School for the Deaf and Blind

Carrie Vonderhaar

Photo credit: Melanie Bess Hansen

Carrie Vonderhaar is the first woman in the long history of Cousteau expeditions to have worked as Chief Expedition Photographer, both topside and underwater. She is also the first woman to have dived in Cordell Bank National Marine Sanctuary on a closed circuit rebreather, and one of the only people to have dived in and photographed all 13 U.S. National Marine Sanctuaries. She was part of Jean-Michel Cousteau's Ocean Futures Society's dive team, which was the first to dive in and document the underwater devastation of the 2010 Gulf oil spill. Carrie is a DMT and volunteers at the Pacific Grove Hyperbaric Chamber in Pacific Grove, California. She lives near the ocean with her husband, Matt Ferraro; daughter, Matilda Dovie; and fur baby, Samantha.

Index

Explore the National Marine Sanctuaries Series With Jean-Michel Cousteau

Based on the famed French explorer's film series Jean-Michel Cousteau: Ocean Adventures, this four-book series is the definitive guide to America's thirteen National Marine Sanctuaries and its one Marine National Monument. Each book conducts a grand adventure through one of the four regions of the National Marine Sanctuary system, combining engaging descriptions, stunning four-color photography, and behind-the-scenes stories from the Ocean Futures Society expedition team. Insightful inquiries into the health of the world's oceans are provided along with an overview of several incredible underwater treasures. Conveying the beauty of the ocean and the specific measures being taken to preserve it, this inspirational collection also features detailed, practical information for planning visits to the sanctuaries.

Explore the Pacific Islands National Marine Sanctuaries

$19.95 US / $29.95 CAN • 192 pages • 7.25 x 9-inch paperback • Full-Color • Over 150 photos • ISBN 978-0-9826940-4-6

Explore the Southeast National Marine Sanctuaries, REVISED

$19.95 US / $29.95 CAN • 208 pages • 7.25 x 9-inch paperback • Full-Color • Over 120 photos • ISBN 978-0-9826940-1-5

Explore the Northeast National Marine Sanctuaries

$19.95 US / $29.95 CAN • 192 pages • 7.25 x 9-inch paperback • Full-Color • Over 120 photos • ISBN 978-0-9826940-3-9

Explore the West Coast National Marine Sanctuaries

$19.95 US / $29.95 CAN • 368 pages • 7.25 x 9-inch paperback • Full-Color • Over 250 photos • ISBN 978-0-9826940-2-2

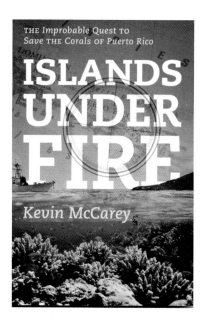

Islands Under Fire

The Improbable Quest to Save the Corals of Puerto Rico

Kevin McCarey

A portrait of an often overlooked part of America—Puerto Rico and the Spanish Virgin Islands—this is the little-known story of how the United States government almost destroyed a pristine coral reef to provide a target for gunners. The author's true and humorous account of his role in this sometimes bizarre tale reveals how locals, politicos, and mariners came together to save a coral reef from certain destruction, and how the need to protect the fragile marine environment can bring meaning and direction to anyone's life, young or old.

$16.95 US / $25.95 CAN • ISBN 978-0-9826940-8-4 (pp)
$24.95 US / $37.95 CAN • ISBN 978-0-9826940-5-3 (hb)
288 pages • 5.5 x 8.5-inch

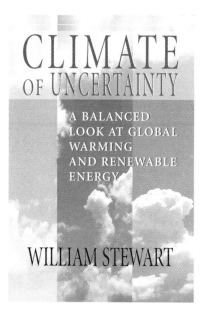

Climate of Uncertainty

A Balanced Look at Global Warming and Renewable Energy

William Stewart

The perfect book for anyone seeking an unbiased understanding of all sides of the climate change issue, *Climate of Uncertainty* explores the topic in a way that all readers can understand. Without taking sides, Stewart examines global warming, renewable energy, expanding populations, and sustainability. He has written to inform, not to persuade, and no viewpoint has been ignored, no opinion belittled simply because it is not widely accepted.

Climate of Uncertainty is a step away from the fray, a fresh and balanced assessment of a debate that is all too often dominated by extremes. This is climate change for the layman, a book about some of the largest concerns facing our world today, and what our options are in dealing with them.

$14.95 US / $22.50 CAN • 192 pages • 6 x 9-inch paperback • ISBN 978-0-9767291-6-7

For more information about our books,
visit our website at www.squareonepublishers.com